James King Smith

TRIAL OF
WALTER GRAHAM ROWLAND

CELEBRATED TRIALS SERIES
GENERAL EDITOR: JONATHAN GOODMAN

published
Trial of Ian Brady and Myra Hindley
Trial of Ruth Ellis
The Archer–Shee Case

in preparation
Trials of Donald Hume
Trial of Graham Young
Trial of Elvira Barney

ALSO BY HENRY CECIL:

Non-fiction
Brief to Counsel
Learn about English Law
(*both illustrated by Edward
    Ardizzone*)
Not Such an Ass
Tipping the Scales

A Matter of Speculation (the
    Case of Lord Cochrane)
The English Judge (the
    Hamlyn Lectures)
Just Within the Law
    (reminiscences)

Fiction
Full Circle
The Painswick Line
No Bail for the Judge
Ways and Means
Natural Causes
According to the Evidence
Brothers in Law
Friends at Court
Much in Evidence
Sober as a Judge
Settled out of Court
Alibi for a Judge
Daughters in Law

Unlawful Occasions
Independent Witness
Portrait of a Judge
Fathers in Law
The Asking Price
A Woman named Anne
Brief Tales from the Bench
No Fear or Favour
Tell You what I'll Do
The Buttercup Spell
I Married the Girl
The Wanted Man
Truth with her Boots on

CELEBRATED TRIALS

TRIAL OF WALTER GRAHAM ROWLAND

With an Introduction
and Edited by
HENRY CECIL

DAVID & CHARLES
NEWTON ABBOT   LONDON
NORTH POMFRET (VT)   VANCOUVER

ISBN 0 7153 7072 3

Library of Congress Catalog Card Number 75-15036

Set in 11 on 12pt Linotype Baskerville and printed in
Great Britain by Latimer Trend & Company Ltd Plymouth
for David & Charles (Holdings) Limited
South Devon House   Newton Abbot   Devon

Published in the United States of America
by David & Charles Inc
North Pomfret   Vermont 05053   USA

Published in Canada
by Douglas David & Charles Limited
132 Philip Avenue   North Vancouver   BC

CONTENTS

THE TRIAL
First Day
Evidence for the Prosecution

Second Day

Evidence for the Defence

Third Day

Fourth Day

THE APPEAL

Evidence for the Appellant

Appendices

ILLUSTRATIONS

Except where otherwise stated, illustrations are reproduced by courtesy of the Chief Constable of Manchester

EDITOR'S NOTE

Those who do not remember the name of Walter Graham Rowland may wonder why his case appears in this series. He was born in 1908, and so was a man called David John Ware. At about the same time or not long before, a woman called Olive Balchin was born. These three people were totally unknown to each other until suddenly in 1946 their paths converged and the result was a unique murder story.

In December of that year Rowland was convicted of murdering Olive Balchin on a bombed site in Manchester by hitting her on the head with a hammer. He was sentenced to death, but shortly after the trial Ware confessed to the crime. Rowland appealed against conviction mainly on this ground, but the Court of Criminal Appeal refused to hear Ware's evidence, and dismissed the appeal, suggesting that it would be better if the Home Secretary ordered an enquiry. Accordingly, at the request of the Home Office, Mr J. C. Jolly, KC, conducted such an enquiry. In the course of it Ware withdrew his confession and Mr Jolly reported that there had been no miscarriage of justice. Rowland was executed two days after this Report.

Four years later Ware tried to kill a woman with a hammer in Bristol. He was found guilty but insane and sent to Broadmoor. So the question arose again. Who killed Olive Balchin? Rowland or Ware? Or someone else?

Owing to the cost of production it is not economic to reproduce the whole of the shorthand note of the trial, but I have included the bulk of the evidence of the important witnesses in the original question and answer form. When some questions or answers, which are of little significance, have been omitted, I have usually put three dots (. . .), but sometimes I have not considered this necessary. When the question and answer form has not appeared to me to be essential, I have sometimes substituted for it a résumé of the evidence. I have had to omit all the speeches of counsel and the summing-up of the learned judge, but I could not have omitted the summing-up if Rowland's counsel, Mr Burke, had not said this in opening the appeal to the Court of Criminal Appeal:

> I have studied with considerable care the summing-up of the learned judge and I am bound to say this, that from start to finish of the case it was conducted with strict propriety and complete impartiality. The summing-up to the jury was perfectly balanced and every point which could have been brought to their notice which tended to favour the interests of the accused was mentioned by the learned judge. I think I ought to say that at once. Furthermore, the evidence which was submitted was, in my respectful submission, admissible and no criticism could be made as to the conduct of the trial on that ground.

INTRODUCTION:
A DOG WITH A BAD NAME

On 16 December 1946 a jury at Manchester Assizes convicted Walter Graham Rowland of murdering Olive Balchin. Thereupon he was asked by the Clerk of Assize if he had anything to say why sentence of death should not be passed upon him according to law. His answer to this question is all the more striking when it is compared with his background.

Rowland was born in 1908 in New Mills, Derbyshire, and left school when he was fifteen. He had respectable parents who occupied the same house ten miles from Manchester for the whole of his life. He was above average intelligence but he could in no sense be described as an educated person. He was employed as an apprentice engineer until he was eighteen, when he joined the Army. After two months' service his parents purchased his discharge. He was then employed for four months as a labourer, when he was dismissed for insolence. In 1927, when he was nineteen, he joined the Royal Tank Corps but after two weeks he was discharged as medically unfit.

On 30 June 1927 he was convicted of causing grievous bodily harm to May Schofield by attempting to strangle her. He was sentenced to three years' Borstal. He was released on licence in 1929 and worked as a labourer from 1929 until 1932, when he lost his job owing to trade depression.

He had a miserable domestic life from the time when he was grown up. He married in 1930 but his wife died ten months later in childbirth. On 5 September 1931 he married Annie May Schofield. I have been unable to find out for certain whether this was the girl whom he tried to strangle in 1927, but I think it very likely that she was. They had a child in 1932, a girl called Mavis Agnes, and in 1934 Rowland was convicted of murdering this child by strangling her.

At his trial for this murder his wife (then Annie May Rowland) gave evidence against him. It was plain from the

11

evidence which they each gave that they cannot have been living very happily together. Just before the murder a warrant had been issued against Rowland for his arrest on a charge of bilking a taxi driver of £3, and Rowland suggested to his wife that he should break open the electricity meter, take the contents (which were very small) and go to Ireland. His wife refused and said that, if he broke open the meter, she would tell the authorities.

It was suggested in Rowland's defence that his wife had murdered the child but the evidence showed that this was not possible. Rowland was convicted and sentenced to death, but the jury recommended him to mercy and he was reprieved. He was released in 1942. I do not imagine that he and his wife ever lived together again but there is no record of any divorce. After his release he joined the Army and served from September 1942 until June 1946.

There were other criminal convictions against him, one of which was for robbery in October 1932. When he was charged with the robbery he was also charged with attempting to commit suicide by drinking lysol. He had attempted suicide on two other occasions when he had been charged, or was about to be charged, with a serious crime. In 1927 he tried to hang himself and in 1934 he took iodine. It is plain from his conduct that he was a man subject to fits of depression, and he obviously hated going to prison.

When I said that his domestic life was miserable I could well have left out the adjective 'domestic', although there is no reason to think that his upbringing by his parents was in any way at fault. He kept in touch with them throughout his criminal career and right up to the moment of his arrest for murdering Olive Balchin his mother was regularly doing some of his laundry for him. He also had an aunt in Scarborough who sometimes did this for him. His letter to his parents before his execution (p. 14) gives an idea of his relationship with them, and his was plainly a case where the existence of home ties did not prevent him from embarking on and persisting in a career of crime.

This was his reply on 16 December 1946 when he was asked if he had anything to say why sentence of death should not be passed upon him according to law:

Yes, I have, my Lord. I have never been a religious man, but as I have sat in this Court during these last few hours the teachings of my boyhood have come back to me, and I say in all sincerity and before you and this Court that when I stand in the Court of Courts before the Judge of Judges I shall be acquitted of this crime. Somewhere there is a person who knows that I stand here today an innocent man. The killing of this woman was a terrible crime, but there is a worse crime been [sic] committed now, my Lord, because someone with the knowledge of this crime is seeing me sentenced today for a crime which I did not commit. I have a firm belief that one day it will be proved in God's own time that I am totally innocent of this charge, and the day will come when this case will be quoted in the Courts of this country to show what can happen to a man in a case of mistaken identity. I am going to face what lies before me with the fortitude and calm that only a clear conscience can give. That is all I have got to say, my Lord.

This speech was delivered from the dock and was not read by Rowland from a piece of paper. My own belief is that it was a genuine extempore speech and that Rowland had not carefully prepared it and learned it by heart. In the course of my enquiries about this case it was suggested to me that Rowland had taken most of it from some speech of Sir Edward Marshall Hall and that he had found this speech in some book in the prison library to which he had access while he was awaiting trial. I very much doubt this. I do not think that this speech reads like a garbled version of something which Marshall Hall once said. My view is that sometimes, when a person was about to be sentenced to death, he was so exalted or inspired by the occasion that words which he would not normally have spoken poured out of him. This was his last performance on the public stage and, consciously or unconsciously, he was going to make the most of it. If I am right in my view that this speech was completely unrehearsed and completely original, I think that many people outside the legal profession, who had not attended the trial and had only heard that speech, would have been convinced of Rowland's innocence. It would be interesting to know if any member of the jury changed his view about Rowland's guilt when he heard it.

Rowland appealed to what was then called the Court of

Criminal Appeal. His appeal was mainly on the ground that after his conviction a man called Ware confessed to the crime and the Court of Criminal Appeal was asked to allow Ware to give evidence before them. They refused and the appeal was dismissed. When it was dismissed Rowland said:

> I am an innocent man. This is the greatest injustice which has ever happened in an English court. Why did you have the man who confessed here and not hear him? I am not allowed justice because of my past.

At that stage the Lord Chief Justice told the officers to remove Rowland, but he clung determinedly to the dock and added:

> It would have knocked the bottom out of English law to have acquitted me and proved my innocence. I say now I am an innocent man before God.

And these are two letters which he wrote just before being hanged. The first one was to his parents.

> Dear Mother & Dad,
>   I understand just how you must have been feeling today when you came to see me for the last time in this world. I ask you to forgive me for trying to cheer you up in the way I did I just had to keep you up or I would have broken down myself. I am sure you will understand Mother and Dad. You know I have told you the truth all along, and you have promised never to doubt, or sease from seeking the truth of my total innocence. The truth will out in God's own time, so just go on with this firm believe in your hearts. Please dont mourn my passing Mother and Dad, I am going into God's hands and into his keeping I shall walk beside you until we meet again in God's Kingdom. I am just going on before. Away from the unjustness and the strain of all the past long days. When you receive this letter I shall be at my rest so do not grieve my passing. Hold up your heads for I die and innocently Christ said on the Cross, for others sin. I die for anothers crime. I tell you mother and dad that before my maker I swear that I am completely innocent of the death of that poor woman. You have each other and those around you to comfort you in your sorrow, hold on to

your faith in God. He will make all clear in His own good
time and way and hold on to your believe in my innocence.
May God Bless you all and comfort you, until we meet again
by His grace in His Kingdom where unjustness is no more
and all shadows flie before His Light.

    With deepest love to you both. Good bye in this World.

Your loving and Grateful Son,

WALTER XXX XXX XXX

The second letter was to a Mr Keymer and reads as
follows:

Mr Keymer
Sir,

    We have come to the parting of the ways. Mr Keymer, I
felt a good deal better when we had had our talk. You see
I was feeling down in spirits because I had just seen my
family, and it is a terrible feeling to know you are seeing
and speaking to them for the last time on this earth. I did
the best I could to ease their feelings. I hope I did make it
lighter for them to bear.

    You know that I have a clear conscience and you have my
sacred word at this time when I am too near to death's door,
that I am an innocent man. I know you will fulfil your
promise to me to go on seeking out the truth of my complete
innocence, no matter what may come or go, no matter how
black they may try to paint me. Keep your faith in my word
to you, Sir, for it is God's truth and nothing can alter that.
My soul will never rest until the truth is found and my name
cleared of this crime. I wish to thank you for all your efforts
on my behalf, the words of cheer you have given me when
the days were dark and long, the helpful advice over so many
of the problems that have beset me during these past weeks
of trial and strain, not only for me but for my family. I
thank you for the visit you paid to my people, it meant a
lot to them. I would like to feel that you would go to see
them again in the future. You would bring something of
contact for me to them and you could talk to them with
the same understanding which would help. They will want
to talk to someone about me, they will need someone to
give them an outlet for their feelings by talking instead of
keeping it all inside them. You would be doing a great
service to me, Sir, and to those near and dear to me. Life
brings some very strange things to some. Why did I not meet

my end in Italy. Why should I come through that to have to die for some other's crime. It is a bitter cup to drink, Sir. My people must live on with the great sorrow of my end with them day after day, a sorrow which is no bringing of mine, a sorrow of which I, like them, am an innocent victim. May God comfort them in their grief over this great wrong that has come to us. Well, Sir, I go to my Maker with a clear and innocent conscience, and the truth of my complete innocence in my soul. I know I shall ever be in your thoughts, Sir. I thank you for all you have done for me and mine. I will close now, with the wish that you are abundantly blessed by the Judge of all Judges. Good-bye Sir.

  I am,
      Yours very Sincerely,
      (Signed) WALTER GRAHAM ROWLAND

One must not attach too much importance to protestations of innocence coming from a condemned man either from the dock or the condemned cell. The man who wants to live clings to the hope of a reprieve, and he feels sure that express or implied admissions of guilt at any time before his execution would be fatal. Many obviously guilty men have protested their innocence right up to the last moment.

But from the point of view of anyone considering *now* whether Rowland was guilty or innocent, the most important words which he used were in the Court of Criminal Appeal when he said: 'I am not allowed justice because of my past.' He might have added: 'I'm a dog with a bad name.'

Rowland had been discharged from the Army in 1946 with an indifferent character, which is hardly surprising as one of his offences while in the Army was attempting to strike a sergeant. After his discharge from the Army he was never in regular work. He lived in hostels and lodging-houses and the police have little doubt that he kept himself mainly on the proceeds of crime. They also believe that he had a sort of love/hate relationship with prostitutes and that, although he consorted with them, he knocked them about. Understandably, the police very much dislike criminals who beat up women.

I do not believe that anyone who has never committed a crime, other than motoring or similar offences, stands in real danger of being convicted of a serious crime of which he is innocent. Indeed it would be a very rare occurrence for him even to be charged with such a crime. The only exceptions to this rule are where a husband is suspected of killing his wife or a wife of killing her husband. And even in the domestic world I can think of only one case where a man who may not have been guilty was convicted of killing his wife. He was William Herbert Wallace and he was tried in 1931. His conviction was set aside by the Court of Criminal Appeal on the ground that no reasonable jury should have come to a conclusion of guilt. I do not think that the case was proved against him and I think it was right that his conviction should have been quashed, but I remain of much the same opinion as the jury who convicted him, though, unlike them, I do not think that the prosecution sufficiently proved its case. You may think a man guilty without being satisfied of his guilt beyond all reasonable doubt. Those who remember the case and disagree with my view will find their own well supported and the story extremely well told in *The Killing of Julia Wallace* by Jonathan Goodman (published in 1969 by Harrap).

But if men and women of good character can feel safe from the awful prospect of being unjustly accused of serious crime, people who have a string of convictions against them are not in that happy position. When a serious crime is reported to the police and they have nothing to go on except the actual circumstances of the crime, they first of all consider the sort of criminal who may have committed it. They then seek out all people in the area of the crime who appear to have the necessary qualifications, and they ask them to account for their movements at the time of the crime.

Most of them, sometimes all, are able to give a satisfactory account of themselves. But sometimes a person, who is completely innocent of the crime, does not like to say where he was on the occasion in question. He may wish to conceal the truth for a variety of reasons, for two in particular. He may be a married man and have been with another woman or he may have been committing another crime. In consequence he lies to the police when questioned, and if the police investigate his statements and find them to be lies, he at once comes under serious suspicion. It is very likely that he will lie again in order to cover up his first lies. As a result

B

sometimes he will be charged with the offence. If his reason
for lying is one which he does not mind telling his wife he
may ask her to give evidence that he was with her at the time
of the crime, or, whatever the reason, she may be prepared
to help him out of loyalty. When he is tried for the offence
she may give her evidence very badly. The jury may be satisfied that the alibi is a false one and then they ask themselves
what possible motive this man could have for putting up a
false alibi unless he was guilty of the crime. And in this way
an innocent man may be convicted.

The police do not want the wrong man to be convicted,
and accordingly the sort of case to which I refer is an
infrequent one, but it does happen.

Rowland was in the Manchester area when Olive Balchin
was killed and I doubt if there was any other man in that
area who by reason of his past was a more likely suspect. No
one but Rowland could be blamed for that, but it is certainly not surprising that he should say that he was denied
justice because of his past after the decision of the Court of
Criminal Appeal, which, for reasons which appear in the
next section, seems to me to have been an unsatisfactory one.

SHIFTING THE BURDEN

The facts of the case are set out in the next section, but the Appeal is dealt with first because it was only on the Appeal that David John Ware became involved, and it is desirable that, when readers are considering the whole of the evidence, they should bear in mind all the time that another man confessed to the crime. For the purpose of understanding the Appeal it is only necessary to know the main ground of it, which was Ware's confession. Rowland sought unsuccessfully to call Ware as a witness before the Appeal Court.

Four years after that Court refused to hear his evidence, Ware attempted to kill a woman, who was a complete stranger to him, in much the same manner as was adopted by the man who killed Olive Balchin. He was found guilty but insane and sent to Broadmoor. I wonder whether the Court of Criminal Appeal would have acted differently if by the use of some Wellsian invention it could have found out what Ware was going to do.

But why did the Court refuse to allow Ware to be called as a witness? There was ample evidence against Rowland, but his case was that the witnesses who had identified him were mistaken and were confusing him with somebody else. Furthermore, he sought affirmatively to prove an alibi. There is now power in the Court of Appeal (Criminal Division) to send a case for a new trial, but when Rowland appealed in 1946/7 there was not. The rules then relating to the power of the Court to hear fresh evidence were as follows. In the first place it would never listen to evidence if it could have been called at the trial. Secondly, it had to be convinced that there were very exceptional circumstances before it would consider the verdict of the jury in the light of fresh evidence.

It was not contested by the Crown that the first condition was satisfied and that Ware could not have been called to give evidence at Rowland's trial. So the Appellant had only to satisfy the Court that there were very exceptional circumstances which justified the calling of Ware.

19

Rowland's solicitors had provided the Court with a copy of three statements made by Ware. The first was a very short one giving practically no details and stating that he wished to confess that he had killed the woman. Within two days of his making this confession the inspector in charge of the Rowland case interviewed him. The inspector formally cautioned him and then took down from him a detailed statement giving dates and places and stating how he came to murder the woman. Subsequently he made an even more detailed statement to Rowland's solicitors. All those three statements were before the Court of Criminal Appeal and, if the basis of them was true, Rowland could not have been guilty of the murder, the identification of him by the witnesses for the prosecution was erroneous and the verdict of the jury ought to have been set aside.

In giving the judgment of the Court Mr Justice Humphreys said:

> Our reason for refusing the application to hear the evidence of Ware was that we were satisfied that the Court of Criminal Appeal is not the proper tribunal to hold such an enquiry. It is no light matter to reverse the finding of a jury who have convicted a person of murder after a trial extending over five days in which twenty-eight witnesses were called. It is obvious that the mere statement of a person such as Ware that the convicted man is innocent because he himself is guilty, even if made on oath, would not justify quashing the conviction of that other person but would only be the beginning of an enquiry which would involve in the light of the new evidence the recalling of many witnesses and probably the calling of several fresh ones.

Subsequently Mr Justice Humphreys went on:

> If we had allowed Ware to give evidence before us and he had persisted in his confession of guilt the court would have been compelled to form some conclusion as to his guilt or innocence and to express that opinion in open court. In effect, therefore, the court would have been engaged in trying not only Rowland, but also Ware and thereby usurping the function of a jury.

In fact, the Court would *not* have been trying Ware. The

only duty of the Court would have been to say whether, if the evidence of Ware had been before the jury, they might have given a different verdict. Had the Court quashed the conviction of Rowland and had Ware subsequently been tried for murder, the Court's finding in favour of Rowland would have been no more prejudicial to Ware than his own confession. If he had persisted in his confession at his trial, the only defence open to him would have been that of insanity. If, on the other hand, he had retracted his confession, he would have had to explain why he had made it and to go on to show where he was at the time of the murder. If the Court of Criminal Appeal had held that Ware's confession made it unsafe to uphold Rowland's conviction, that fact would not in my view have seriously prejudiced Ware's trial. What would have prejudiced Ware's trial would have been his own confession.

It is quite true that, had the Court heard Ware's evidence and had he persisted in his confession and not been shaken in cross-examination, it might well have been necessary to call further evidence to see whether his confession might have been a true one. Unquestionably this might have imposed a considerable burden on the Court of Criminal Appeal and, in my view, what the Court did was to transfer this burden to the Home Secretary, who transferred it to one of His Majesty's counsel.

Strangers who have had nothing whatever to do with a crime do from time to time confess to it. Sometimes they are insane, sometimes they are exhibitionists, sometimes they hope to get free travel to the place where the offence is being investigated and sometimes it is difficult to find any reason for their behaviour. But occasionally someone does confess to a crime of which he is guilty, after another person has been convicted of it. Ware had made three statements, the first to the governor of a prison, the second to a police officer and the third to a solicitor, and in two of them he gave a detailed story of how and why he committed the crime. I should have thought that those facts plainly constituted a very exceptional circumstance which made it incumbent upon the Court to hear his evidence.

In dismissing the appeal Mr Justice Humphreys said:

Finally, we are not unmindful of the fact that there exists an authority in the person of the Home Secretary, who has far wider powers than those possessed by this Court, who is not bound as we are by rules of evidence, and who has all the necessary machinery for conducting such an enquiry as is here asked for.

The Home Secretary did in fact order such an enquiry and it was conducted by Mr J. C. Jolly, KC. Mr Jolly was appointed on 21 February 1947 and he made his report on the 25th. He had an unenviable task. Rowland was waiting in the condemned cell and Mr Jolly rightly considered that he must not be kept waiting any longer than was absolutely necessary. To have conducted such an enquiry in ninety-six hours without making any mistake was almost impossible. A mistake was in fact made in the statements put before Mr Jolly and he did not notice it. He reported on 25 February that Rowland's conviction did not constitute a miscarriage of justice, and Rowland was hanged on 27 February.

I shall deal in detail with the enquiry later, when readers will already have learned all that is known of the crime and the evidence called at the trial. At the moment it is only necessary to say that during the course of the enquiry Ware withdrew his confession and said that it was untrue. That leaves three questions. Was his confession a genuine one? Was his retraction a genuine one? If he had given evidence before the Court of Criminal Appeal, would he have retracted his confession or persisted in it? Mr Jolly gave his answers to the first two questions. No one can answer the third.

THE CASE AGAINST ROWLAND

Here now is the story of the murder and of the arrest and trial of Rowland. I shall first of all deal with matters which were not in dispute between the prosecution and the defence.

Olive Balchin was about thirty-eight or forty when she was killed and she had probably seen better days. Her body was identified by a man called Angood from Hertfordshire, who was a retired coal-wharf manager. He had known her for about nine years and last saw her about three years before the murder. The circumstances in which he knew her were never disclosed. It is conceivable that he was a relative, as it seems rather odd that the police should have gone as far away from Manchester as Cheshunt in Hertfordshire to find someone to identify her, if he was not a relative. Hers must have been a sad life because she had reached a stage when she was apparently prepared to have intercourse with men on bombed sites for as little as ten shillings a time plus some tea and cakes. At the time of her death she had been living in the Manchester Corporation's women's hostel for nearly two months and very little money was found on her. Her few possessions were sent to her next of kin, who is believed to have been a parson then in Belgium. She was not a bad-looking woman and why she had been reduced to a life of prostitution is unlikely to become known.

Olive Balchin had a horrible death which must in any event excite deep sympathy, but, if Rowland was guilty, I find the story of their lives' end a particularly sad one. Each of them was about the same age, each of them was hopelessly unsuccessful in life and cannot have known much happiness, each was almost penniless and in effect they destroyed each other on a bombed site in Manchester. But *was* Rowland guilty?

At about 11 am on Sunday, 20 October 1946, Olive Balchin's dead body was found upon the site of a bombed building at the corner of Deansgate and Cumberland Street, Manchester. She had been killed by repeated blows on the head and face with a hammer, which was found near to the body. On the very same site was found a piece of paper in which it subsequently turned out that the hammer had been wrapped on the previous day.

At this stage of the case the police were wholly unaware that Rowland knew Olive Balchin. As soon as possible after the discovery of the body they caused a picture of the hammer to be advertised in the Press, and a shopkeeper called MacDonald at once came forward and said that he recognised it. He was able to identify it quite positively by reason of the facts that the number '4' was stamped on the metal and that the shaft of the hammer was not the normal shaft for a hammer of that kind. He said that on Saturday, 19 October, at about 11 am he bought the hammer from a man called Rawlinson who was a boot and shoe repairer. The hammer was not an ordinary hammer but what is called a leather-dresser's hammer. MacDonald had sold only one of these before. At about 5.40 pm on 19 October a man came into his shop and pointed to the hammer in question and asked its price. MacDonald told him that it was 3s 6d and asked him why he wanted it. 'Oh, just for general purposes', said the man. 'Well, it's no good for that', said MacDonald. 'You couldn't use it to drive in a nail, for example.' 'It will suit my purpose', said the proposed purchaser, and bought it.

MacDonald described the man as aged about 28–32, 5ft 7in or 5ft 8in in height, medium build, very pale face, thin features, clean-shaven, quiet-spoken, no hat, white soft collar and shirt, dark tie, dark suit and a dark fawn cotton rain-coat. He said that he was of clean and respectable appear-ance. He added that the man put the hammer, which had been wrapped up in the brown paper, into his raincoat pocket, went out of the shop and walked towards the city.

On 20 October, Norman Mercer, the licensee of a public house in Deansgate, was told about the incident and tele-phoned to the police to say that at about midnight on 19/20 October he had seen a couple quarrelling near the site of the murder. He was taken to the mortuary and he recognised the dead body of Olive Balchin as the woman whom he had seen quarrelling with the man. Later in court he agreed that she was 'in a sorry state' when he identified her. Although the inspector in charge of the case said that it would not be easy to recognise her from a photograph of her in that condition, Angood recognised her battered face two days after she was murdered, although he had not seen her for three years. Mercer also recognised her coat, which had noticeably large buttons (see the photograph on p. 33). He described the man as being a man of 'proportionate' build and said that he had a dark suit on and appeared to have dark hair.

Two or three days later Mrs Copley, a waitress in a café just off Deansgate, was questioned by the police and said that a woman, whom she subsequently identified by photographs reproduced on p. 52) as Olive Balchin, had come into her café between half-past ten and eleven pm on 19 October with another woman and a man. She described the man as having dark hair and a fresh complexion and said that he was wearing a dark suit.

At this stage the police had no idea who the murderer was and they took their normal course in such a case, which was to make routine enquiries around the lodging-houses and hostels, where they suspected that the sort of man who had committed a murder like this might reside.

While they were making these enquiries complaint was made to the police by a man, who had stayed at one of the hostels, that he had lent a raincoat to a man called Roland (which he spelt without the 'w') and that it had never been returned. Sergeant Trippier, who was a Manchester City Police officer concerned in the murder enquiries, decided to find out something more about this man called Roland. As a result he was told about Rowland and learned that he frequented the Manchester area and had a criminal record, which included at least two offences of violence. He reported this to the officer in charge of the case, Inspector Stainton, and in view of the fact that Rowland's physique as described in his record was consistent with the description which had been given by the three witnesses, he decided that it was worth while bringing him in for questioning.

Accordingly, the inspector sent Sergeant Blakemore and Detective Constable Nimmo at about 11 pm on 26 October to fetch Rowland from the Services' Transit dormitory where he then was. Detective Constable Nimmo knew Rowland, as he had been a police officer concerned with a case of warehouse-breaking of which Rowland had been suspected some months before. He was tried for that offence at Manchester Quarter Sessions and put on probation.

The officers went to the hostel and found Rowland asleep. They told him to get dressed and to come to police headquarters to be interviewed by Inspector Stainton. Rowland did not make any objection to going but this was probably because he thought that the police had power to make him.

There was a dispute as to what Rowland actually said when the police officers woke him up, but one thing he agreed that he did say was: 'Is it about that coat?' This question was not answered and it is one of the odd things about the trial that the history of that coat does not appear to have been seriously pursued by the police either before or during the trial. The coat was a raincoat and Rowland said to the police and at the trial that he had borrowed it from an American, who was known as 'Slim', and that he had given it back to him within the hour. For some reason the prosecution did not challenge his statement, although it is absurd to think that, if he had borrowed the coat for less than an hour, any complaint that it had been stolen would have been made to the police. The importance of the coat was this. One of the strong points in Rowland's favour was that there was no blood on his clothes, but the prosecution would have had a complete answer to this if it could have shown that he was wearing a raincoat, as MacDonald said he was. Although Mercer and Mrs Copley did not see him in a raincoat, if, as the prosecution alleged, the murder was premeditated, he could have put the raincoat with the hammer on the bombed site before he took Olive Balchin there. But this was never suggested by the prosecution, and except for Rowland's question, 'Is it about that coat?', the raincoat goes out of the picture after the man who bought the hammer left MacDonald's shop.

Rowland was taken to the police station and questioned there by Inspector Stainton. There is some dispute about some of the questions and answers at that interview and at the moment I will refer only to the statements which Rowland agreed at the trial that he had made.

He stated that he had known Olive Balchin for about eight weeks, that he had had intercourse with her twice, once on a bombed site but not the one where she was found murdered, and once in a doorway. He said that he thought that he had VD and he wanted to find out if she had given it to him. He said that he had a pride in his body and that it was a blow to him to find that he had VD. He said that he had seen Olive Balchin on 18 October at Littlewood's Café, Piccadilly, Manchester, that he had bought her cakes and tea and that before he left her he said that he would see her the following night. He told the police that, had he been sure that she had given him VD, he would have strangled her.

Referring to the injuries which Olive Balchin had sustained he said that, if she had given him VD she deserved all she got and that things like that didn't happen to a decent woman and that the person who did it did it for a cause. Referring to the hammer he said: 'It is possible the hammer was got to do a job with. I was not going to do a job that night. The fact that I went home proved that.'

Rowland made other statements at this interview about his whereabouts at the time of the murder but he did not then tell the police the address of the place where at the trial he swore that he had spent the night. He did not accept some of the police evidence about his statements on the subject of his whereabouts, so I have omitted them for the moment.

At 3 pm on Sunday, 27 October, Rowland was put up for identification with ten other men and told that he could stand anywhere that he liked. After the identification parade he was asked if he had any complaint about it and he said that he had not. At the parade Mrs Copley, with some hesitation, picked him out as the man she had seen in company with Olive Balchin and the other woman between 10.30 and 11 pm on 19 October. When she came on to the parade she walked along the line of men, hesitated in front of Rowland and then walked to the end of the line. She then went back to Rowland, put her hand on his shoulder and said: 'I'm not certain but I think this is the man.' At the trial she said that he had been in her café once or twice before the night of the murder, and Rowland admitted that this was the case. He denied, however, that he had been in the café on the night of 19 October.

At the same parade MacDonald identified Rowland as the man to whom he had sold the hammer on the day of the murder. He looked along the line of men and went straight up to him and put his hand on his shoulder.

At 4.30 pm on 27 October Rowland was formally charged with the murder of Olive Balchin and said that he was not guilty.

It can fairly be claimed on Rowland's behalf that he made some very frank admissions to the police. Why should he have done that if he was a guilty man claiming that he was innocent? Why did he not just deny that he had ever heard of Olive Balchin? Or, if he thought that other witnesses could prove that he did know the woman and that it would, therefore, be dangerous to deny that he knew her, why did he make wholly unnecessary admissions against himself? Why did he state that he would have strangled her if she had given him VD? Why did he state that he had said that he was going to see her 'tomorrow night'? No one could have proved either of these matters.

At a further identification parade Mercer identified Rowland. He did not at first identify him but said that he would like the men on the parade to turn side-face. As soon as that was done he did identify him. And he said that that was how he saw him on the night of the murder.

So far, all the matters to which I have referred were not in controversy. Apart from his general allegation that the three witnesses were mistaken, Rowland relied upon an alibi as far as two of them were concerned but he could not rely upon this defence in respect of MacDonald's evidence. This was that the hammer was bought from him at about 5.40 pm on the night of 19 October. Rowland's statements as to his movements on that day were as follows.

He said that on the Saturday morning he went up to Old Trafford to do some business.

I met a girl called Edith. We went on a tram to a café in Salford not far from the Ship Hotel and had a cup of tea. She had no money and I had no money. I left her. I told her that I was going to a post office. I had arranged to meet some of the boys to get some money. I met the boys in Liston's bar and had a few drinks with them. We went to Yates's and had a few more. At 3 o'clock I left them and went to the café where I saw Edith. She started creating and so I left her and went down town again. I knocked about town and had a wash. I went to the post office for a parcel I was expecting but it wasn't there so I decided to go home for it. I got a bus at Lower Moseley Street to New Mills, where I arrived at about a quarter past eight.

To have done this he would have had to catch the 6.15 bus at Lower Moseley Street. MacDonald's shop was in Downing Street, Ardwick, and Rowland had ample time to get from the café where he had left Edith to MacDonald's shop and then back to Lower Moseley Street in time to catch the 6.15 bus. He did not say exactly when he left Edith at the café but it is plain from what he did say that he had time on his hands because he said that he 'knocked about town and had a wash'.

Mrs Copley's evidence was that she saw Rowland between 10.30 and 11 pm on 19 October in the café where she worked, and Mercer's evidence was that he saw him quarrelling with Olive Balchin at about midnight just by the bombed site, where the murder took place. Rowland's evidence was that he was nowhere near the place of the murder at that time and that he arrived at a lodging-house at 81 Brunswick Street, Chorlton on Medlock, Manchester, at about 11.15 pm. He said that he was either in that house or very close to it until next day.

In addition to this evidence the Crown sought to rely upon a certain amount of technical evidence, but this came to very little. They proved that there was material in the turn-ups of Rowland's trousers which was similar to the sort of material which was found on the bombed site. They proved that there were certain hairs on his jacket which could conceivably have belonged to Olive Balchin. They might have been his own and, if he had been near enough to Olive Balchin to get hairs on his suit, it would have been remarkable that there was no blood on his suit as well. The Crown did, however, prove that there was a trace of blood upon the side of the heel of one of Rowland's shoes. There was enough blood to establish that it was human, but not enough to determine its group. Rowland's explanation of this blood was that he might have got it when he stepped into somebody's spit or, alternatively, when he was cut whilst he was being shaved in the police station. Although his explanation seems somewhat improbable it does not seem impossible and not much weight was added to the prosecution's case by the presence of the blood on the shoe. It was undoubtedly a point in Rowland's favour that there was no trace of blood on his suit and that his fingerprints were not on the hammer or the paper.

Other matters relied upon by the prosecution, which were in dispute, consisted of statements which it was alleged that Rowland made, first when he was woken from sleep at the lodging-house and secondly during his questioning by Inspector Stainton.

The disputed statements which he is alleged to have made were as follows. When he was woken up at the lodging-house, Detective Constable Nimmo said that Rowland sat up in bed and when he saw him said: 'You don't want me for murdering that fucking woman, do you?' Rowland denied that he mentioned the woman at all. He said that he used the word 'fucking' in connection with some remark about Nimmo, whom he knew, troubling him again.

At the police station, when questioned by Inspector Stainton, he is alleged to have said when asked to account for his movements:

> I am admitting nothing, for it's only a fool's game to do that. I can account for where I was. I was at home at New Mills when she was murdered. I didn't come back to Manchester that night.

Inspector Stainton then said, 'Do you care to tell me where you stayed on the Saturday night, the 19th?', and Rowland said, 'Have you seen my mother?', to which Inspector Stainton replied that he had not. Rowland is then alleged to have said:

> Well, I did come back to Manchester. I got a lift in a car and then went to a pub for a drink. I didn't go into Deansgate. I stayed in the Ardwick district where I had a bit of supper and stayed at Grafton House, Hyde Road. I didn't get in until after one o'clock.

The inspector then said: 'It will be necessary for me to

make enquiries at Grafton House to prove your statement', upon which Rowland is alleged to have said: 'Well, I didn't stay there. I stayed at 36 Hyde Road. I only stayed there one night.'

Whatever the truth of the matter, Rowland may have made a genuine mistake when he referred to Grafton House. Grafton House is in fact 67 Hyde Road and there is no doubt that on the day after the murder, that is on 20 October, Rowland did stay at 36 Hyde Road. He may well have stayed at Grafton House on a previous occasion, and, as it was also in Hyde Road, have mixed up the two addresses.

As far as 36 Hyde Road is concerned, however, he said that when he first told the police that he had stayed there on the night of the murder he genuinely thought that he had, but subsequently realised that he had not done so and had stayed the night in Brunswick Street. He said that he could not give the number of the house or the name of the person who owned it and that he deliberately did not tell the police about it because he thought that they would not believe him, in view of the fact that he could only remember the name of the street. Subsequently he ascertained through his solicitor that it was 81 Brunswick Street, the lodging-house of a man called Beaumont. And that is the place where he said he was at the time of the murder, although admittedly he did not tell the police that when he was questioned by Inspector Stainton.

The case then against Rowland consisted mainly in:

1 His admissions to the police.
2 Identification of him by MacDonald, Mercer and Mrs Copley.
3 The fact that he never stated where he spent the night of 19 October when he was being questioned by Inspector Stainton.
4 That at the interview with Inspector Stainton he said that he reached the place where he did stay the night at any time from 12.45 am to 1.15 am.

ROWLAND'S DEFENCE

Rowland's defence was that, although he knew Olive Balchin and had said that he would see her on the night of the murder, he did not intend to keep that appointment, he did not keep it, he never saw her that night and he did not kill her.

He said that on the evening of the murder he arrived at his parents' house in New Mills at about 7.30 pm, changed his shirt and underclothes, replacing a brown-striped shirt and collar with a blue shirt and collar, and put on the same suit again. He left his parents' house at about 9.20 pm and got a bus at 9.30 pm, intending to go to Manchester. The bus stopped at Stockport at Mersey Square. He got off and went into the Wellington Hotel for a drink. He said that just before closing time at 10.30 pm he had gone to the lavatory and when he came out and into the bar again he saw two police officers walking out through the door.

He went out shortly afterwards and caught a bus going towards Manchester. He got off on the Manchester side of Ardwick Green shortly after 11 pm. He asked a soldier where he could find a bed for the night and was directed to 81 Brunswick Street. He had in fact stayed there before but did not realise it until the landlord opened the door. He signed the visitors' book at 81 Brunswick Street, and went out again shortly afterwards for about ten minutes to try to buy a soft drink. The landlord lent him a key but was still up when he got back. He then went to bed. He spent the next night, that of 20 October, at 36 Hyde Road. After that he went to the Salvation Army hostel where he spent the nights of the 21st to the 24th inclusive.

He said that he had never been into MacDonald's shop and never bought a hammer from him. He said that he had not been in the area of Deansgate for any part of the evening or night of 19 October. He had been to the café where Mrs Copley worked, but not on that day.

His evidence that he was at the Wellington Hotel, Stock-

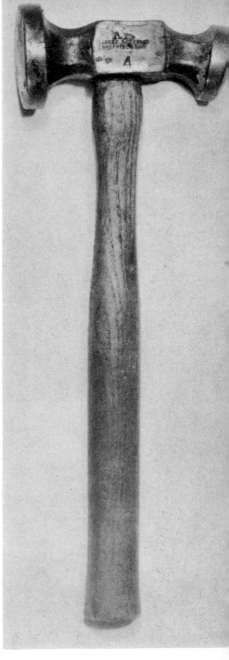

Page 33 (*left*) Model wearing Olive Balchin's coat and hat; (*right*) the hammer

Page 34 (*left*) Walter Graham Rowland; (*right*) David John Ware

port, between 10 and 10.30 pm was corroborated by the fact that he had seen two police officers pass through the bar there at about 10.30 pm and by one of those police officers, who gave evidence that he and a colleague had in fact passed through the bar at that time on that day, although they did not see Rowland. Rowland's evidence was also corroborated by two witnesses who gave evidence in the Court of Criminal Appeal and, if Rowland had been allowed by that Court to call Mrs Coppock, the wife of the licensee of the Wellington Hotel, she would probably also have corroborated his evidence that he was in their bar at the time he said. His application to call Mrs Coppock was refused by the Court because his solicitor had interviewed her before the trial and therefore she could have been called to give evidence at the trial.

Rowland's alibi at the Wellington Hotel, however, was not of vital importance, because, if he was there at 10.30 pm, he could probably have got into Manchester by bus by 11 pm and, if he got a lift by car, very much sooner. Stockport is about seven miles from the middle of Manchester.

The vital part of Rowland's alibi was his allegation that he stayed the night of the murder at 81 Brunswick Street and that he arrived there at about 11.15 pm. In this he was corroborated by the landlord of 81 Brunswick Street, Frank Beaumont, who said that Rowland arrived at about 11.15 pm to 11.20 pm, that he went out for a very short time to get a soft drink, and that when he, the landlord, went to bed at about 11.40 pm, Rowland was in the house. He said that Rowland slept in the middle room on the ground floor and that, although theoretically it would have been possible for Rowland to go out and come back without his knowing it, it would be most improbable that he could do this. In any event, if in fact Rowland was in the house at 11.40 pm it is almost certain that he did not commit the murder.

Beaumont produced his registration book, but unfortunately this showed 19 October as the day of Rowland's departure. Beaumont said that the 19th was a mistake for the 20th.

Rowland's main defences may be summarised as follows:
1   His alibi.
2   The absence of blood on his clothes.

c

3 The absence of his fingerprints on the hammer or wrapping paper.

4 His frank admissions to the police.

5 Criticisms of the identification by the three main witnesses. I deal with these in detail on pp. 42–5.

But, although these were Rowland's defences at the trial, it must always be remembered that Ware confessed to the crime and subsequently attempted to commit a similar crime. Accordingly, before coming to a conclusion on the matter, it is important to consider Ware's confession, retraction and subsequent crime very carefully indeed. However strong the evidence against Rowland, if there was a reasonable possibility that Ware was the murderer, there must be a doubt about Rowland's conviction.

DAVID JOHN WARE

David John Ware was born in 1908 at Skewen in Glamorgan. I have been unable to find out anything about his upbringing, but it is clear that he became a petty criminal. He started off in 1931 with a very stupid attempt at blackmail, threatening to accuse a man, of whom he knew nothing, of being unfaithful to his wife. He was trapped without difficulty and sentenced to twelve months' imprisonment with hard labour. When he came out from prison in 1932 he married and had two children. In 1937 he deserted the three of them. He was called up for military service in August 1942 but was discharged on medical grounds in July 1943. He was then stated to be suffering from manic-depressive psychosis. In 1943, 1945 and 1946 he was sentenced to short terms of imprisonment for offences of dishonesty.

If Ware was still suffering from manic-depressive psychosis in 1946, his mental condition could have accounted either for his murdering Olive Balchin or for his wrongly having confessed to her murder. The fact that he attempted murder in 1951 shows that his condition appears to have continued up till then, and it therefore seems to be plain that the man who confessed to Rowland's alleged crime was himself a potential murderer.

When Ware attempted to kill the woman in 1951, he adopted very much the same procedure as had been adopted by Rowland. In the afternoon he bought a hammer, having decided to kill a woman, any woman. He said that he had the urge to kill someone so long as it was a woman. With the hammer in his pocket he went to the Downs in Bristol where he saw a woman sitting on a seat. He got into conversation with her and suggested that they went for a walk. During the walk they sat on the grass and he then decided to kill her. After the first blow the head of the hammer flew off and he 'laid into her with the shaft'. He then ran away but later gave himself up and confessed that he was the person who had attacked the woman.

The great difference between the two cases was that Rowland admittedly had a motive for killing Olive Balchin, whereas the only reason why Ware attacked his unfortunate victim was that he was mad.

But the first question to be considered is whether Ware could have killed Olive Balchin. As his confession and retraction are so important I have included the whole of Mr Jolly's Report as an appendix.

In the course of his enquiry Mr Jolly questioned Ware about his three confessions. Eventually Ware admitted that they were false and said that he had not committed the murder. He signed a further statement in which he gave details of his movements on the day preceding the murder, on the day of the murder and on certain subsequent days. After Ware had withdrawn his confession of murder Mr Jolly arranged for the three witnesses, MacDonald, Mercer and Mrs Copley, to attend an identification parade in which Ware was simply one of eleven men.

Each witness failed to recognise any of the eleven men as resembling Rowland or the man they had seen. They then attended a further confrontation with Ware only. All of them stated positively that Ware was not the man. Readers will be able to judge from the photographs on p. 34 whether there is any likeness between the two men.

Mr Jolly sets out in his Report the steps which he took to try to verify the truth of Ware's retraction of his confession. Unfortunately in the retraction itself either Ware himself or Detective Inspector Hannam, who took it down, made a mistake. In my view it was a perfectly obvious mistake and its origin can be plainly seen if all the statements made by Ware are looked at. Mr Jolly and Inspector Hannam did not notice it. They rightly thought that Ware was referring in his statement of retraction to 19 October as being the vital day, but, if his statement is looked at literally, it refers to the 20th. Mr Sydney Silverman, in a book about the case, spends about seven pages trying to destroy the value of Mr Jolly's Report, mainly by treating this mistake as though it were not one. It is an important matter and therefore I must deal with it in detail. It will be easier for readers to follow the argument if they first read each of the appendices to Mr Jolly's Report (see pp. 154–64).

In his first detailed statement Ware said that he had stolen money from the Salvation Army hostel in Stoke and that he left Stoke on Friday, *18 October* (my italics), and arrived in Manchester at about 7.30 pm. He said: 'I met a girl and stayed the night with her in some part just outside the city. On Saturday morning I left her and wandered around.' He then describes how on Saturday 19 October he decided to buy a hammer and bought one. Then he deals with his meeting with Olive Balchin (whom he called Balshaw) and of his murdering her at about 10 pm. He says that he slept the night at Stockport in a lodging-house. He goes on to say that on Sunday 20 October he went to Buxton and to Chapel-en-le-Frith and stayed the night at an institution. On Monday, the 21st, he hitch-hiked to Sheffield and surrendered to the police for the stealing of the money at Stoke Salvation Army hostel.

This last statement was made to Inspector Stainton. As a result of it Ware was questioned by his own solicitor, who wrote out the second confession statement. That statement resulted from questions and answers. Whenever this is done, what is written down is often a combination of the question and the answer. The important day in everybody's mind was 19 October, the day of the murder, but Ware had said in his original statement, as I believe quite correctly, that he arrived in Manchester from Stoke-on-Trent on 18 October. However, when he was questioned by the solicitor, the latter wrote down the 19th as the day on which Ware arrived in Manchester from Stoke-on-Trent instead of the 18th and then went on to deal with what he did on the day after his arrival. What he did on the actual day of his arrival was irrelevant to the enquiry. Ware then goes on in the statement to deal with the buying of the hammer, which in the original statement he said was bought on 19 October, and with his movements after the murder and his eventual surrender.

After he had said that his confession was untrue and when he was making a statement about what he said were his real movements, there was the same confusion between the 18th and the 19th of October. He said that 'on the 19th October I was in Manchester, arriving by train from Uttoxeter at 7.30 pm or thereabouts'. It is quite plain that what he meant to say was that on 19 October he was in Manchester, having arrived by train from Uttoxeter at 7.30 pm on the 18th. He dealt in detail with his movements on the day when he arrived in Manchester and referred again to his picking up a girl and spending the night with her. Having spent the night with her he said that they left the house on the next day a bit after 10 o'clock. It is quite plain that the next day was in fact the 19th and not the 20th. The 19th was a Saturday and the 20th a Sunday. Ware referred to various things which he could not possibly have done on a Sunday, eg going into Woolworth's.

After dealing with his movements in detail he said that he went to a lodging-house in Stockport. He said that he did not know the name of the lodging-house or the street, but he described where it was and the people who managed it. In particular he mentioned an old man in charge of the book-ings. As a result of this description Inspector Hannam went to a lodging-house at 7 Great Egerton Street, Stockport, and interviewed the proprietress and an old gentleman who was in charge of the bed bookings. They confirmed Ware's state-ment that he stayed there on 19 October and said that he arrived between 11.15 and 11.30 pm.

Once the confusion between the 18th and the 19th is cleared up, it appears that Ware spent the night of 19 October from about 11.15 or 11.30 pm at 7 Great Egerton Street, Stockport, having arrived there about half an hour before Mercer saw Olive Balchin alive. Ware himself in his confession put the time of the murder at about 10 pm. It is therefore plain that, if Mercer's identification of Olive Balchin is correct, it was not Ware who killed her.

Mercer identified her not only by her face but by her coat with the large buttons. It would be an odd coincidence if the woman whom Mercer saw was not Olive Balchin but was wearing a similar coat with large buttons.

Ware was a man who had at first toyed with the idea of being in the dock for murder and of being hanged, and who finally became obsessed with it. He told a prison doctor that he had falsely confessed to a murder in Edinburgh. In the end, his obsession became so great that, having failed to get the authorities to hang him, he hanged himself in Broadmoor on 1 April 1954.

After reading Mr Jolly's Report and after correcting the

mistake about the dates, my view is that Ware could not have committed the murder. It therefore becomes necessary to examine the evidence in Rowland's case again to see if he was rightly convicted. The most important matter to consider is the identification by the three witnesses.

THE IDENTIFICATION

There is a good deal of talk today about the way in which an identification parade should be held in order to prevent mistakes and unfairness. It should be remembered that in Rowland's case no complaint whatever was made against either of the parades. He himself agreed at the first parade that it was fair and his solicitor was present at the second parade. But because a parade is held fairly it does not mean to say that a mistake cannot be made. One thing is very important and that is that the witness who has come to identify the suspected person should not have seen a photograph of him before. Both MacDonald and Mercer had seen photographs of other criminals but they each swore quite definitely that they had not seen a photograph of Rowland. Mrs Copley was not asked if she had seen a photograph of Rowland.

I will take each of the identification parades in turn.

First of all, MacDonald's. He said that he had a good memory for faces. If his evidence is correct, he had a conversation with the man to whom he sold the hammer which could well have made the occasion stay in his memory. He identified Rowland at once, and later on, when the enquiry was being held by Mr Jolly, he said quite definitely that Ware was not the man.

One point that was raised against MacDonald was that he had failed to identify Rowland at the magistrate's court until the prisoner was told to stand up. MacDonald's version of what happened was as follows. Rowland was not in the dock but was sitting by his solicitor. When he looked round the Court MacDonald could not see him but there was a man who, he said, had his head bent down over the desk in front of him so that the witness could not see his face. He asked that the man should stand up, so that he could see his face. Rowland then stood up and he at once identified him.

Rowland's account of what happened was that when MacDonald could not see the man in Court, counsel for the prosecution asked Rowland to stand up, whereupon he was identified.

Now Mr Hinchcliffe, Rowland's solicitor, was present in Court on that occasion and counsel for Rowland said that he would be called to give his version of what happened, but he never was called. This must mean that he accepted Mac-Donald's version of what happened. It is quite inconceivable that Rowland's two counsel and his solicitor should allow a point like that to go by default.

Another point taken against MacDonald's identification (and Mercer's and Mrs Copley's as well) was that they all said that Rowland had dark or darkish hair and that it was brushed back and had oil or grease on it. But Rowland and his mother said that he never greased his hair, and he called evidence to show that he had refused a gift of a bottle of brilliantine once when it was offered to him by his mother and that he gave it to his brother. In Court it appeared that Rowland's hair was not dark. It was not very fair but it certainly could not be described as dark or darkish. What the witnesses said about that was that, when hair cream or oil is applied to hair, it makes it look darker. That these three witnesses were right about this appears to have been almost conclusively proved by the evidence of a fourth witness. This was Captain Reid of the Salvation Army. He was in charge of a hostel where Rowland admittedly stayed several nights. There was no dispute that Captain Reid and Rowland knew each other at the time of the murder. Captain Reid's evidence was that Rowland came to stay at his hostel on 21 October and that he stayed there until 24 October. Tickets were issued to him for each night of his stay and these tickets were found upon him when he was arrested. Captain Reid said that Rowland came to the hostel between 10.15 and 10.30 am on 21 October. He was then asked:

How did his hair appear to you that day?

Dark.
Was it dry or——?
Well greased—hair cream.
Dark and greased?
Dark and greased.
How was it brushed? If at all?
Brushed back.

It will be seen from the photographs of Rowland (p. 34) that he took trouble over his appearance and in particular his hair, and it seems to me that the point about the hair was destroyed by Captain Reid's evidence.

The next point against MacDonald's identification was that he said that Rowland was wearing a white shirt and collar, whereas Rowland's evidence that he was wearing a brown-striped shirt and brown-striped collar was corroborated by his mother.

Rowland was vigorously defended by two counsel and a solicitor and, if there had been anything in this point, they would either have arranged for the actual shirt and collar to be produced or have accounted for its absence. In any event, MacDonald saw the man for only a few minutes and could have made a mistake about his shirt and collar, or, alternatively, the shirt and collar could have been so faded as to look white to him. The unexplained failure to produce or account for the absence of the shirt seems to me to rob the point of any value.

The next witness was Mrs Copley and undoubtedly she was not quite certain in her identification. Naturally this was relied upon by defence counsel and furthermore it was pointed out that, as she had seen Rowland on at least two previous occasions, she ought to have been able to identify him more easily rather than less. It was also put against her that she described Olive Balchin as a girl when she was in fact thirty-eight. There is little or nothing in that point because, when she was asked how old the young girl was, she said, 'about my age. About thirty-eight'.

The third witness was Mercer. He did not immediately identify Rowland at the parade but asked for the men to stand with their faces sideways to him. When this was done, he identified him. He said that that was how he had seen him when he had seen him quarrelling with Olive Balchin.

These three people were respectable people who did not know each other or Rowland or Olive Balchin and admittedly had no reason for being biased against Rowland when they gave their evidence, except perhaps that they thought him guilty of the crime. They were all warned of the importance of the occasion and they must have all realised that their evidence, if believed, might result in Rowland being executed. It is difficult to believe that any of them wanted an innocent man to be hanged. So at any rate they must themselves have believed that their evidence was correct. But they could still have been mistaken.

CRITICISMS OF THE VERDICT

Since Ware's conviction in 1951 a number of people have impugned the verdict of Guilty against Rowland, both on the ground that, even on the evidence before them, the jury should not have convicted, and also because Ware's confession and subsequent crime make it plain in their view that Rowland was almost certainly innocent. The late Mr Sydney Silverman, MP, Lord Paget (formerly Mr R. T. Paget), QC, Mr Arthur Koestler and Mr Leslie Hale are some of those who have expressed these views. Their main contentions and the arguments on the other side are as follows.

1 *The fact that the three vital witnesses all gave the colour of Rowland's hair as dark when it was shown in the dock that it was not.*

I have already dealt with this on pp. 43–4.

2 *MacDonald's identification of Rowland in the Police Court.*

I have already dealt with this on pp. 42–3.

3 *MacDonald stated that Rowland was wearing a white shirt and collar whereas Rowland and his mother said that it was a brown-striped shirt and collar.*

I have already dealt with this on p. 44.

4 *The three vital witnesses gave differing descriptions of Rowland.*

It would have been very surprising if they had not done so. Some people are more observant than others. Had they all given precisely the same description one would have suspected some collusion. As it was, they put his age at 28–38, his height and build approximately as it was and they all said that he was wearing a dark or blue suit.

5 *Olive Balchin was too injured to be convincingly identified by Mrs Copley and Rita Leach.*

These witnesses were shown the photographs which appear on p. 52 and readers can judge for themselves whether there would have been any difficulty in identifying Olive Balchin from them.

6 *Rowland's account of his movements on 19 October before he went to his parents' house at New Mills are inconsistent with his going to MacDonald's shop.*

This is just not correct. According to his own statement he had ample opportunity of going there before he caught the bus for New Mills.

7 *Mrs Copley referred to Olive Balchin as 'a young girl', although she was in fact thirty-eight.*

When Mrs Copley was asked how old the 'young girl' was she said 'about my age. About thirty-eight. She looked young'. She also referred to Rowland, both when she said she saw him in the café and when she saw him at the dock, as the 'young man'.

8 *The insubstantiality of the technical evidence relating to the blood on the shoe, to the hairs on the coat and to the debris in the turn-ups of the trousers.*

Neither prosecuting counsel nor the judge laid emphasis on any of these points. I agree that the hairs and the debris should be disregarded and that, although the blood on the shoe is curious, it is too slight to be of any serious significance.

9 *The judge was rather inclined to suggest to the jury that the evidence about Rowland seeing the police going through the bar of the Wellington Hotel was irrelevant.*

I agree that this is a fair criticism and do not think that the judge fully appreciated the effect of the evidence.

I was once told a story by my father of a sentry at Buckingham Palace who was charged with sleeping at his post at midnight. His defence was that he was awake and that he heard Big Ben strike thirteen. It was found that the clock had struck one too many and the man was acquitted. It is quite true that he might have learned from somebody else that Big Ben had struck thirteen, just as Rowland might have learned from somebody else or have known from experience that policemen did go through the bar of that hotel at that particular time on a Saturday night, but nevertheless in each case the fact that it really happened was evidence to support the story of the man in question.

But even if Rowland was at the Wellington Hotel, Stockport, at 10.30, he could still have reached Deansgate before 11 pm. It is quite true that Mrs Copley said that he came in with two women at 10.30 pm, and left at about 11 pm, but she might be a little wrong about her times. However, if one assumes that she was right about the times and that she saw somebody else at her café and not Rowland, that does not mean that Mercer and MacDonald were also wrong. There was no evidence whatever to discredit MacDonald's story except his description of Rowland's hair. That point was completely disposed of by the evidence of Captain Reid.

10 *Rowland's alibi.*

I have already dealt with the Wellington Hotel part of the alibi.

As for the alibi at 81 Brunswick Street, Rowland himself said originally by implication that he arrived there long after 12 midnight. He never explained how he came to make such a mistake if Beaumont was right in saying that he arrived at about 11.15 pm on 19 October. Beaumont's registration book was in a very unsatisfactory state and in fact showed Rowland as *leaving* on 19 October. Beaumont said that this was a mistake for the 20th, but the 19th as the date of his arrival could equally have been a mistake for the 18th. This would make much more sense, as Beaumont said that Rowland told him when he arrived that he was after a building job 'on the following day'. If he arrived on the 18th, the following day was a Saturday, but, if he arrived on the 19th, the following day was a Sunday, and Rowland agreed that he was not going to look for work on the Sunday. The strong probability is, therefore, either that Rowland arrived at Brunswick Street on the Friday and left on the Saturday or that he arrived about 1 am or after on the Sunday morning.

As readers will not have an opportunity of seeing Beaumont's registration book, I think it is desirable to include a description of it by counsel for the prosecution. This is what he said:

On the left-hand side of the page appears the date of arrival. On the right-hand side appears the date of departure and, certainly at first sight, it appears to record that Rowland arrived on the 9th October and departed on the 19th. The prosecution do not, however, suggest that he stayed there for ten days, and that he arrived on the 9th. But that is what the book appears to record and I merely make this comment, that you will probably think, when you look at this book closely, that it is a singularly inaccurate record, and one from which you could not draw any satisfactory conclusion as to dates. The next two dates after the entry showing the arrival on the 9th or 19th, whatever it is supposed to be, are two entries, the dates of which are smudged. They are smudged so as not to be properly legible and, if you look back through the book, they are probably the only two seriously smudged entries in the whole book, and are a singular and remarkable coincidence, if it is one, and they appear to record the date of arrival of the next two visitors at this establishment as being either the 15th and 16th, or the 25th and 26th. If, in fact, they record arrivals on the 15th and 16th, it would mean that the entry relating to Rowland's arrival would be unlikely to be the 19th because it would then be out of date . . . I invite you, in particular, to look at the date of the entry showing the arrival of somebody, whose name is illegible, on the 16th or the 26th, as the case may be. If you turn over the page and look at the back of it, you will see that the '2' of the '26th' has come through on to the back, whereas the '6' has not, suggesting that the '2' was possibly written in after or inked in more heavily later . . . If, as the defence suggest, these figures here are '19' and not '9', if the book does in fact show that Rowland arrived on the 19th and left again on the 19th, because there is no doubt as to the leaving date—the '19' is written quite clearly—it means that, if that is accurate, he arrived sometime after midnight on the 18th—that is after midnight on the Friday . . . and left again the same day, perhaps after his breakfast on the Saturday morning. That would fit in with 19th arrival and 19th departure. If that is not so, then the book is inaccurate somewhere, and you may think that the inaccuracy is this. You may think that, in fact, he stayed there on the Friday night, the night of the 18th, and, when the book showed he was leaving on the 19th, that is quite accurate, and that the date of his arrival has been wrongly entered, and should read the 18th.

11 *Ware's confession and his subsequent crime.*

I have dealt with this in the section on Ware. He was unquestionably mad and, having confessed to the murder of Olive Balchin and having taken a considerable part in the enquiry conducted by Mr Jolly, he may well have become obsessed with that particular method of killing a person and so adopted it himself when he decided to give way to his insane desires.

Page 51 (*above*) Deansgate, looking towards Cumberland Street, showing blitzed site; (*below*) the body of Olive Balchin

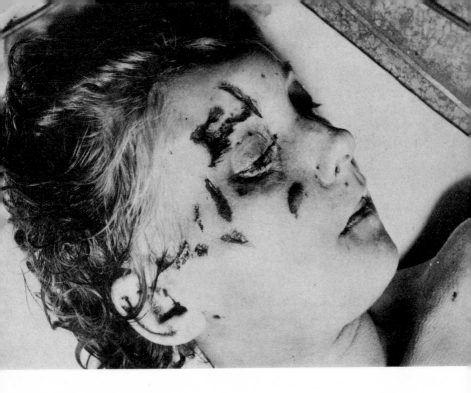

Page 52 Olive Balchin: (*above*) photograph taken at the mortuary; (*below*) retouched photograph.

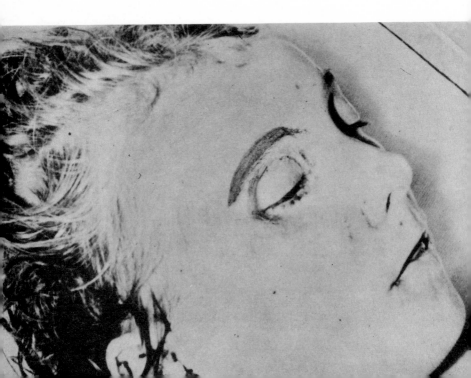

CONCLUSION

I have come to the clear conclusion that, in spite of Ware's
confession and in spite of the fact that four years later he
attempted to commit a similar crime and in spite of the criticisms which have been made of the verdict, the case of
Rowland calls for no further enquiry. He was plainly guilty.
Undoubtedly there were coincidences in the lives of Rowland and Ware. They were born in the same year, joined the
Army in the same year, had unhappy married lives, were
both in very reduced circumstances, living from hand to
mouth, and they both had suicidal tendencies. These are
actual facts. The only coincidence which is not conclusively
proved to be a fact is that each of them should murder or try
to murder a woman in the same way. This is undoubtedly a
very curious circumstance and can be claimed to be an
unlikely coincidence, but it is nothing to the incredible
coincidences involved if Rowland was innocent.

Perhaps the most striking one is this. Rowland said that
he would have strangled Olive Balchin if she had given him
VD. He had in fact got VD. On the day of the murder he
thought that he had it and he suspected her of having given
it to him. Now when Rowland said, 'I would have strangled
her', it was no figure of speech. At least twice in his life he
had strangled, or tried to strangle, someone. He had said that
he would meet Olive Balchin on the night of the murder. In
these circumstances it would have been extraordinary if Ware
or anyone else had come along that night and killed her. And
it would have been more amazing still if MacDonald, who
knew nothing of all this, should be wrong when he said that
he was sure Rowland was the man to whom he sold the
hammer.

But the coincidences do not stop there. Mercer knew no
more of Rowland's association with Olive Balchin than
MacDonald, but he must have been wrong too when he
identified Rowland, if it was in fact another man whom he
saw with Olive Balchin. And Mrs Copley must have been

wrong as well. And Rowland himself must have been wrong when he said that he reached his lodgings on the night of 19 October after 1 am.

Those who criticise the rightness of the verdict refer to the dangers of convicting upon evidence of identification and to the cases where people have been wrongly identified, and in particular to the case of Adolf Beck. But Adolf Beck did not know the women who identified him. Rowland did know Olive Balchin. I find it impossible to believe that three respectable people who did not know each other, who did not know Rowland or Olive Balchin, who were wholly unaware that Rowland suspected Olive Balchin of giving him VD and had said that he would meet her on the night of 19 October, who did not know that Rowland was a strangler and who had no reason whatever for not telling the truth, were all wrong when they identified Rowland.

The fact that Rowland was a strangler may make some people wonder why he chose to use a hammer on this occasion. Presumably the reason was that he had to murder her in public, as he had no place of his own to which he could take her. He might well have thought that it would be difficult to start to strangle someone in public without there being a grave danger of at least one scream being heard. A very heavy but unexpected blow from a hammer would be unlikely to result in a scream. Certainly no one appears to have heard Olive Balchin scream.

There are some further matters to which it is worth calling attention. One is only a small one but the others are more important.

The small one is this. Rowland was asked in cross-examination why he did not stay at his parents' house on the evening of 19 October. He had nowhere to sleep in Manchester, he had very little money and the next day was Sunday. He had no work to go to and there seemed no reason why he should not stay with his parents. When he was asked the question: 'Why did you not stay at home at New Mills?' his answer was: 'I should think that would be obvious'. The cross-examination continued as follows:

Would you answer my question?—Yes, I will. Because I have a great respect for my mother and my home. Feeling as

I was feeling and thinking I had something wrong with me, I did not want to stay and use one of their beds.

When you say thinking you had something wrong with you, you mean thinking you had venereal disease?—I do, yes.

I suggest that this answer was untrue. Rowland was sending his laundry to be dealt with by his mother. If his reason for not staying at the house was because he suspected that he had venereal disease it is difficult to understand why he continued to send her his laundry to wash.

Another matter is this. I have said in Rowland's favour that he made serious admissions against himself when he need not have done so. For some curious reason this behaviour seems to have been part of his nature. Just before his arrest for the murder of his child he did much the same thing. He had been detained at New Brighton on a charge of bilking a taxi driver. A police officer said that he was going to telephone to Stockport, where a warrant had been issued for Rowland's arrest upon a similar charge. Upon being told this, Rowland said: 'If you ring up the Mellor police they will tell you something more serious than that'. Mellor was the place where he had left his child dead. At the trial he sought to explain away his statement by saying that at Mellor he had broken open the electricity meter and had stolen 6s and that was what he meant by 'something more serious than that'. As the Stockport bilking charge was for £3, no doubt the jury were not prepared to accept his explanation. It is almost as if making admissions had a fatal fascination for him, even though he ultimately wanted to be acquitted.

An even more important matter is one which shows that, when Rowland was charged with a serious offence, although he would make unnecessary admissions before the trial, he would perjure himself at the trial in an effort to be acquitted. In re-examination by his own counsel in Olive Balchin's case, he was asked:

It has been put to you too that you have an uncontrollable temper. You have stated on oath that you have.—I have.

Without saying what they are, have you done things in the course of your life in temper for which you are sorry?—Yes, I have.

With regard to those things which you have done in your temper and for which you are sorry, have you ever planned them out hours ahead?—Never.

Why? Have they been done on the spur of the moment?—In the heat of the temper, sir.

I do not want to go any further than this. Are these things, or some of them, in the knowledge of the police force?—They definitely are.

By his answers to those questions Rowland must have been admitting that his convictions for murder and causing grievous bodily harm were justified, as these were the only offences of violence in his record. At his trial the jury were not allowed to know about his previous convictions. But when one is considering whether a miscarriage of justice has occurred and whether an innocent man has been hanged, one is entitled to go into all the facts. The fact that Rowland denied his guilt on oath in the earlier cases is relevant to the value of his oath when he was seeking to avoid conviction for the murder of Olive Balchin.

It is also of some relevance to refer to what he said after the jury had convicted him of the murder of his child and had recommended him to mercy. In reply to the formal question whether he had anything to say why sentence of death should not be passed upon him according to law, he said: 'If I was guilty, my Lord, I should not deserve mercy. I still say now that I am an innocent man as far as this charge is concerned'. But he was not, and no one suggests that he was.

People may disagree with my conclusions, though I have no doubt of them. But it is difficult to forget his moving speech before being sentenced to death for Olive Balchin's murder. It is true that in his evidence he is inclined to refer too much to his conscience and to God (a tendency of guilty men, who feel that a mere assertion of innocence lacks conviction), but it is odd that a brutal man was able to write, like one of the Elizabethan poets, of 'His Kingdom where unjustness is no more and all shadows flie before His Light'. It is extremely sad that this is not the quality in Rowland for which he will be remembered.

THE TRIAL

AT THE

MANCHESTER AUTUMN ASSIZES

on

12, 13, 14 and 16 December 1946

BEFORE

MR JUSTICE SELLERS
(and a jury)

THE KING

versus

WALTER GRAHAM ROWLAND

MR BASIL NIELD, KC, and MR BAZIL WINGATE-SAUL (instructed by the Director of Public Prosecutions) appeared for the Crown

MR KENNETH BURKE and MR H. OPENSHAW (instructed by Messrs T. H. Hinchcliffe & Son) appeared for the accused

FIRST DAY   *Thursday, 12 December 1946*

THE CLERK OF ASSIZE: Walter Graham Rowland?

THE PRISONER: Yes.

THE CLERK OF ASSIZE: You are indicted and the charge against you is murder, in that on or about 20 October 1946 at Manchester you murdered Olive Balchin. How say you, Walter Graham Rowland, are you guilty or not guilty?

THE PRISONER: Not guilty, sir.

THE CLERK OF ASSIZE: Walter Graham Rowland, the names that I am about to call are the Jurors by whom you may be tried; if you object to them or to any of them, your time to make objection is when they come to the Book to be sworn and before they are sworn, and you will be heard.

(Seven members of the Jury were sworn, and before the eighth member was handed the Book he said: 'I do not believe in capital punishment'. He was removed and replaced by another. Then this member and the remainder of the Jury were sworn.)

THE JUDGE'S CLERK: If anyone can inform my Lords the King's Justices or the King's Attorney General ere this Inquest be taken between our Sovereign Lord the King and the Prisoner at the Bar of any murder, felony or misdemeanour committed by the Prisoner at the Bar let him come forth and be heard, and all persons bound by recognisance let them come forth prosecute and give evidence, because the Prisoner at the Bar now stands on his deliverance, or they shall forfeit their recognizances.

THE CLERK OF ASSIZE: Members of the Jury, the Prisoner at the Bar, Walter Graham Rowland, is indicted, and the charge against him is murder, in that on or about 20 October 1946 at Manchester he murdered Olive Balchin. Upon this indictment he has been arraigned and upon his arraignment he has pleaded that he is not guilty and has put himself upon his country, which country you are, and it is for you to inquire whether he be guilty or not and to hearken to the evidence.

MR NIELD *opened the case for the Crown.*

EVIDENCE FOR THE PROSECUTION

HENRY MARTIN, *police-constable in the Manchester City Police, examined by* MR WINGATE-SAUL, *said that he was the official photographer to the Manchester City Police Force. He stated that he took photographs at the scene of the murder and various other photographs relevant to the case. He produced the photographs which he had taken.*

HAROLD ROWBOTTOM, *detective-constable in the Lancashire County Constabulary, examined by* MR WINGATE-SAUL, *said that he was a member of the staff of the Home Office Forensic Science Laboratory at Preston. He said that he received from the Director of the Laboratory the coat and hat which had been worn by Olive Balchin and which was put on another woman after Olive Balchin's death and photographed.*

JAMES ACARNLEY, *of 89 Cumberland Street, Manchester, examined by* MR NIELD, *said that on 20 October about 11 am his attention was called to the body of Olive Balchin by two boys. The body was on a bombed site at the corner of Cumberland Street and Deansgate. He went to the police.*

THOMAS JAMES ROSS, *police sergeant in the Manchester City Constabulary, examined by* MR NIELD, *said that he went to the scene of the murder. He described the position of the woman and the hammer and the piece of paper at the scene of the murder.*

WILLIAM ANGOOD, *of 25 Albury Ride, Cheshunt, Hertfordshire, examined by* MR WINGATE-SAUL, *said that at 3.45 pm on 21 October 1946 he went with Inspector Stainton to the mortuary at Platt Lane, Manchester, where he identified the body of Olive Balchin as someone whom he had known three years previously. He had known her for about nine years and she was aged 38 or 40. He last saw her three years ago in Hertfordshire.*

SARAH BAYLEY, *of Ashton House, Corporation Street, Manchester, examined by* MR WINGATE-SAUL, *said that she was the resident manageress of the Manchester Corporation women's hostel where the dead woman, whom she called Olive Balshaw* [sic] *had stayed.* [No doubt it is from that statement that the Press got the wrong name.]

The last time she saw her alive was on 13 October, the Sunday before she was killed. Olive Balshaw had stayed at the hostel every night from 25 August until 18 October, except for one night when she was away.

DR CHARLES EVANS JENKINS, *of 8 St John Street, Manchester, examined by* MR NIELD, *said that he was a doctor who made the post-mortem examination of Olive Balchin. He said that she was aged 40–50, yellow hair turning grey. He said she had received numerous blows by some blunt instrument on the right side of the face and that the bone round the right eye had been broken and the brain was protruding. The right cheek bone was broken and there were other injuries to the head. He said that the injuries could have been caused by the hammer which was shown to him. He said there was no trace of venereal disease.*

In cross-examination by MR BURKE *he agreed that you would expect to find blood on the clothing of the man who had inflicted those injuries. He said he would be surprised if there weren't any blood but that it was not impossible. He was asked if it was improbable and he said 'Yes, it is improbable'. He said that it would have been necessary to hold the hammer in a very tight grip to inflict the injuries described.*

EDWARD MACDONALD, *of 6 Wesley Street, Chorlton on Medlock, Manchester, examined by* MR NIELD, *said that he was a licensed broker and had a shop at 3 Downing Street, Ardwick.*

MR NIELD: I want you to remember if you will the afternoon of 19 October last.—Yes, sir.

On that afternoon had you in your licensed broker's shop a hammer for sale?—I had several.

Would you look at Exhibit 5?—Yes, that is the hammer I sold.

When was it placed in your shop window?—At 3 o'clock in the afternoon.

What sort of hammer is it?—It is a leather-dresser's hammer.

Now you say that on that day you sold it?—Yes.

Who came into your shop?—A man, sir.

Can you tell us at approximately what time he came in?—Yes, sir. At about twenty to six.

Would you look round this court and see if you see the man?—Yes, sir. That is the man in the dock.

Did you have any conversation with him?—Yes, sir.

What was said?—When he bought the hammer, sir, he never seemed to know what it was for so I was a bit inquisitive and I asked him after he had purchased the hammer and I had wrapped it up, 'Excuse me,' I said, 'What d'you want this hammer for?' Which I never did to anybody being an exceptional tool. He didn't seem to know what the thing was and it was no good for ordinary use.

When you asked him what it was for, what did he say?— He said, 'General purposes'. I replied to him that it was no use for that. It wouldn't knock a nail in. So he turned round and said, 'It will suit my purpose'.

Was anything said about its normal use?—No, nothing was asked otherwise. I just said, 'O.K.' and gave it to him and 'Goodnight' and out he went.

How much did he pay for it, Mr MacDonald?—Three and six, sir.

You said that you wrapped it up for him?—Yes.

Where did you get the paper from to wrap it up?—Off a roll of paper I have in the shop, sir.

MR JUSTICE SELLERS: Crepe paper, you call?—Crepe paper, yes sir.

MR NIELD: Would you look at Exhibit 7?—The same paper, sir.

Is that part of the roll which was in your shop for wrapping purposes?—I cannot swear to the paper, sir, there may be others, but this looks like the piece of paper it was wrapped in because of the way it's torn. You can only tear it across the grain, you cannot tear it the other way ...

Is there any particular part of that hammer or mark upon it from which you can identify it?—Yes, sir. There was a '4' on it. There was a '4' on the bottom of it. On the bottom of the head, sir.

On the bottom of the head?—Yes, sir. And this is not the original shaft that was in the hammer: it's not the original shaft that should be in the hammer. It's a new shaft that has been put in. That is why I recognised the shaft as the same shaft which was in the hammer head that I sold.

When the man who bought the hammer left your shop did you see which way he went?—He went towards the city, sir.

On Sunday, 27 October, eight days later, did you attend at the Bootle Street Police Station?—Yes sir, I did.

At an identification parade?—Yes, sir.

Were there a number of men on the parade?—Yes, sir, there were.

Who did you identify as the purchaser of that hammer?— The man in the dock, sir.

Cross-examined by MR BURKE:

Have you ever given evidence in criminal cases before?— No, sir.

Never?—Never.

A licensed broker is a man who buys and sells all kinds of things?—Yes.

Second hand?—Yes, sir, correct.

You remember quite a lot about this hammer, do you not? —Yes, sir, I do.

You remember that there was a figure '4' on the bottom when it was in your shop?—Yes, sir.

You remember, do you not, that when it was in your shop it had a shaft different in type from the sort of shaft which such a hammer should have?—Yes, that was the hammer shaft that was in my shop but they are generally fitted with a different type of shaft.

And you remember that it was a leather-dresser's hammer? —Yes, sir.

You remember, too, do you not, according to your evidence, the appearance of the man to whom you sold it?— Yes, sir.

And the conversation which you had with him?—Yes, sir.

Have you ever mentioned a word about that conversation in your evidence before?—No, sir.

Why not?—Because it wasn't asked for.

Was it asked here?—No, sir, I was about to say it but it didn't come up, sir.

Now remembering all those things about the hammer and about the man who bought it, are you able to tell my lord and the members of the jury when you acquired it?— Yes, sir.

Where?—I acquired it at eleven o'clock on 19 October, Saturday.

Do you know the man from whom you acquired it?—No, sir. I went to his house to buy them.

To buy them?—To buy that hammer with other tools.
This hammer was with other tools I bought.

What sort of a man was he in appearance?—A slim man,
sir. Tallish.

D'you think you'd recognise him if you saw him again?—
I think so. I might do. I don't know.

Did anybody else buy a hammer from your shop that day?
—No.

You frequently sell hammers?—I sell plenty of hammers,
sir, yes.

How long before that day was it when you sold a hammer
before of any kind?—Well, I sell hammers as a rule every
day of the week.

Every day?—Every day hammers of some sort or another.

I am asking you whether you can remember when it was
you sold a hammer previously to that?—I sold one on the
Friday, sir . . .

What sort of hammer was that?—A joiner's hammer.

Is the man who bought the hammer personally known to
you?—No. A passing customer.

Could you describe him to the jury? . . .—He was an
ordinary working man.

It's a very general description, isn't it?—Yes.

What was he like?—What d'you mean? In age or features?

Working men differ, don't they, like other kind of men?—
Yes, they do, but I don't take particular notice of everybody
who buys a hammer.

But you seem to have a very good memory, don't you, with
regard to the types of hammer which you sell?—Oh yes.

You've just said that you remembered that the type of
hammer you sold before was a joiner's hammer?—Yes, sir,
quite right.

You remember that clearly, do you not?—Yes.

Can you remember—working man or no working man—
what the appearance of that man was like? To whom you
sold that joiner's hammer?—Yes, sir, to a certain extent.

What?—What I saw of him. I was not taking any particular notice of the man's features or anything like that because
I had no conversation with him bar selling the hammer and
the hammer is an ordinary hammer which is used in the
ordinary way.

Do you remember giving evidence in the Police Court?—I do, sir.

And was the accused represented by this gentleman here, Mr Hinchcliffe, the solicitor?—Yes, sir.

Where was Rowland in that court? . . . —He was sat down amongst a lot of police officers and barristers and barristers' clerks. Of course I don't understand much.

He was sat amongst a lot of police officers?—He was sat on a form in the front and there was police officers and barristers there.

I must put it to you, Mr MacDonald, first that he was not seated among a lot of police officers?—Well, there were police officers on the bench. They were at this end of the bench.

Was he seated on the left of his solicitor, in front of the dock, as it might be *there*? Just think.—He was seated on the left, sir. Yes.

You identified him in the Police Court, did you not?—Yes.

As the man to whom you sold the hammer?—Yes.

Were you first asked by prosecuting counsel in the Police Court to look round the court to see if you could see the man?—Yes, sir.

With the hammer?—Yes, sir.

The dock was empty, was it not?—Yes, sir.

Did you look round the court carefully?—Yes, sir.

Did you first of all say on your oath in the Police Court that you couldn't see the man to whom you sold the hammer?—Yes, sir. I was a bit flustered and the man had his head bent.

Do you swear that?—Yes.

He had his head bent?—He had his head bent on the table as if he was writing.

You noticed him then, did you?—Then I noticed the man.

I put it to you that he did not have his head bent.—Well, I say he did, sir.

I suggest to you that you looked straight at him full in the face.—No, sir.

Did you not?—No, sir. Not the first time.

The first time?—No, sir.

I suggest to you that having done that and having been asked by counsel whether you could see the man in court you said that you couldn't.—I did the first time, sir.

The first time? The second time you did identify him, did you not?—I did, sir.

Tell my lord and the jury, is this what happened? Did counsel for the prosecution ask you if you had attended an identification parade?—Yes.

Did he ask you whether you had picked out at that identification parade the man who had bought this hammer from you?—Yes, sir, he did.

Did you say you had?—Yes, sir.

Did counsel for the prosecution then say to Rowland or tell Rowland to stand up?—No, sir. He asked me to have a further look round the court to make sure the man was not there.

Do you swear that?—Yes, sir. And he appeared in the same position, the same man. The other man's face was up, this man's face was down. And I said, 'Will you ask that man to stand up?'

I'm going to put to you what I say happened. You realise, of course, the grave consequences of a case of this kind?—I do, sir.

I suggest to you this. That when counsel for the prosecution asked you whether you could see the man in court to whom you sold the hammer and when you said, 'No', prosecuting counsel then asked you whether you had attended an identification parade. You have agreed with that, have you not?—I did, sir.

And picked a man out. Did he then ask Rowland to stand up?—No, sir, he did not.

And pointing straight at Rowland when he was standing up, said, 'Is that the man?'—No, sir, he did not.

I am calling Mr Hinchcliffe, if necessary, to give evidence about this matter.—I do not mind, sir. I can only speak the truth.

According to your evidence today, you said to this man something like this. 'What do you want to use this hammer for?'—Yes. I said, 'Excuse me, but what do you want this hammer for?'

Did you ever tell that to the learned stipendiary magistrate in the Police Court?—I did not.

That you made a remark of this kind?—I made the remark but I don't know whether it was put in evidence, sir.

Do you say that you did tell the learned stipendiary magistrate that you had asked the man who bought this hammer?
—I was not asked, sir.

What are you going to use this hammer for?—I was asked no questions like that at all. I was just asked to identify him.

You have been asked no question here today to elicit that reply, have you?—No. Because I was told that this must not be spoken until later.

You told the court today that the man replied, 'For general purposes'.—Yes, sir, he did.

You said 'It's no use for that'.—Yes, sir, I did.

'It will not knock a nail in'. That is what I said.

The man who bought the hammer said, 'It will suit my purpose'.—That is what he said, sir.

When did you first tell the police that conversation had taken place?—Well, it was imparted in Bootle Street.

What?—It was imparted to the detective in Bootle Street.

A lot of people buy hammers at your place of business?—Not these sort, sir.

Hammers of one kind or another?—You don't get many of these hammers. I've only had two of those in my lifetime, sir.

You only make a police statement once in a lifetime, don't you?—Yes, sir.

You're selling hammers every day?—I don't know what that's got to do with it.

Perhaps the members of the jury do. Did you give a description of the man to the police?—I did, sir.

To whom you sold the hammer?—I did.

Before this man was ever arrested?—Yes.

This woman is alleged to have been killed on the night of 19/20 October. You realise that?—Yes, sir, I realise that.

When did the police first come to you about this hammer?
—The police never came to me.

When did you first go to the police?—I notified the police myself. I saw a photograph in the paper of the hammer—the hammer I had sold on the Saturday.

When did you inform the police that you had sold a hammer?—At tea-time on the 20th. Monday, the 20th.

At tea-time on Monday?—Yes. It would be the 21st.

When did you see the photograph of the hammer displayed in the paper?—At five o'clock at tea-time. When I went home for my tea.

Did you then give a description of the man to whom you sold the hammer?—Yes, sir, to the best of my ability.

Was it an accurate description in your opinion?—So far as I could remember, sir, yes.

Did you say he was on the dark side?—I did, sir.

Look at this man there. He is not on the dark side, is he? —No, sir. But he had his hair plastered down with grease that night. His hair was plastered with grease. I noticed that. That is probably what made him look dark.

Did you mention that to the police in your description which you gave on the Monday?—No, I cannot tell you what I mentioned to the police.

Did you tell the police on the Monday that his hair was plastered down with grease?—Yes, I told them his hair was greased.

I am suggesting that you could put as much grease as you like on that man's hair and he would not look dark.—It looked dark in my shop . . .

You told the police he was a dark man, did you not?—On the dark side, I said.

Did you say he had a pale face?—I did, sir.

This man has not got a pale face, has he?—Well, he appears pale to me now.

D'you think so?—Yes.

Did you say that he looked ill?—I said he looked very pale.

Did you say that he looked ill?—No, sir, I did not.

Do you remember giving evidence at the Police Court?— Yes, sir.

Do you remember saying to the learned stipendiary, 'I said he had a pale face and may have said he looked ill'.—Not as I remember, sir.

Was the deposition read over to you when you had given your evidence?—Where, sir?

Was the evidence that you had given written down in the Police Court when you were giving it?—Yes, sir.

Was that which was written down read over to you?—Yes, sir, it was.

Did you listen carefully to what was said when it was read over?—I'm a little bit on the deaf side, sir.

Did you ever tell the learned stipendiary or his clerk that you were deaf and couldn't hear?—I did not tell them I was deaf.

Whether you heard it or not, you put your signature to it? —Yes.

In a serious matter of this kind, you wouldn't put your signature to a document, would you, without knowing what it contained?—Well, I did. I heard all the contents of it. It was sufficient for me to hear.

Did you also tell the police that the man who bought the hammer spoke in a quiet tone of voice?—I did, sir.

Then you later were taken to an identification parade?— Yes, sir.

Had you been shown certain photographs before you attended that identification parade?—No, sir.

What?—I had not been shown then. I had been shown photographs but not the particular time I was called for the identification parade.

I want to make my question quite clear. Prior to being brought to that identification parade, had you been shown any photographs?—I had been shown plenty of photographs, sir.

Who by?—By the Detective Department in Bootle Street.

Plenty of photographs?—Yes, sir. Hundreds.

Hundreds?—Yes, sir.

Hundreds? Is that right?—Yes, sir. Hundreds of photographs.

When you were shown these hundreds of photographs prior to the identification parade, were you shown a photograph of this man?—No.

How d'you know?—I never recognised his photograph anywhere there.

How do you know you were not shown a photograph of this man among those hundreds that were displayed for your view?—Well, there was nobody like him.

Pardon?—There was no photograph of him there, sir.

How do you know?—I was trying to find him for the purpose of identifying him.

Were you looking for a man on the dark side with a pale face who looked ill? Is that what you were looking for when you went through those photographs?—No, sir.

When you were shown these photographs, were you shown them in this way? That they were put before you as pictures of the men who might possibly have committed this crime? —No, sir.

If that was not the reason, will you tell my lord and the jury why you were shown these hundreds of photographs?— To try and see if the man was in the photographs.

Pardon?—To see if I could identify any of the photographs as the man I sold the hammer to.

Did you pick out any man in those photographs?—Did I pick out any man?

Yes. That's what I asked you.—No, sir.

Did you pick out any man in those photographs who might be like the man who bought the hammer at your shop?—Yes, sir, I think one or two.

Did you tell the police when you picked out these one or two photographs that they represented the person who might be the man who bought the hammer?—No, sir.

Did you put some photographs on one side or anything like that?—Yes, sir.

What for? Why?—To have a look at them again, sir.

Was that because you were not sure?—Sir?

Was that because you were not sure as to whether or not they were photographs of the man who bought the hammer at your shop?—I was sure they were not photographs of the man. But there was a similarity between them. That is all.

When this man came into your shop—the man who according to you bought the hammer—had he got a hat on?—No, sir.

That being so, it would be easy to see whether he was a dark or light haired man? Would it not?—His hair looked dark that night, sir, whatever he may have done to it. The man's hair looked dark but of course he is not in my shop a week; he is only in three or four minutes.

Did his hair appear dark when you picked him out on the identification parade?—No. But I never forget a face.

I am talking about the identification parade. Did his hair appear dark when you picked him out on the identification parade?—No. It looked as though it had been washed, sir.

So it did not appear dark?—No, sir.

Did it appear light?—Yes, on the light side.

E

Not on the dark side, as you suggested to the police?—No, sir, it was dark when I saw it.

Do you remember what sort of a collar he was wearing?—Pardon, sir?

Do you remember what sort of a collar this man was wearing that bought the hammer at your shop?—Yes, sir, I think I do.

What sort of collar?—A blue collar. A striped collar.

A striped collar?—Yes.

A striped blue collar?—Did you swear in your evidence before the magistrate that he was wearing a white collar? Just think.—Yes, I did, sir. The second time I was thinking about.

What?—I was thinking about the second time when I identified him at the parade.

Just let me remind you of your words. Did you say this before the magistrate. 'As far as I could see, the man was wearing dark clothes and a white collar'?—Yes, I said it looked very clean, sir.

Did you say a white collar?—Yes, sir, I did.

So why do you say now that the collar which you saw him wearing was blue?—I'm thinking of the second time when I identified him at the identification parade.

Pardon?—When I identified him on the identification parade he was wearing a blue collar . . .

I will make the matter clear, if I may. When a man came along to your shop to buy a hammer, what kind of collar was the man wearing? D'you remember that?—What kind of collar?

Yes.—A white collar, sir, so far as I could see . . .

Are you sure he was wearing a white collar?—As far as I could see, sir.

'As far as I could see.' Are you sure of this? Whatever sort of collar it was, it certainly wasn't a blue striped collar?—Yes, sir.

Was he wearing anything above his suit of clothes—the man who bought a hammer?—Pardon?

Was the man who bought the hammer wearing any outer garment above his suit of clothes?—He had a raincoat.

Was it open or was it buttoned up?—It was open, sir.

And you say he placed the hammer in his pocket?—Yes, sir.

Did he place it in the pocket of his suit of clothes or in the pocket of his raincoat?—As far as I could see, he put it in the pocket of the raincoat. I was not taking much particular notice of where he put the hammer.

You were not taking much particular notice? I'm suggesting to you, Mr MacDonald, that you are utterly mistaken when you say this man bought that hammer at your shop?—No, sir. I'm not mistaken. That is the man who bought the hammer from me.

I am suggesting to you that although he was staring you in the face at the magistrate's court, you were unable to pick him out until he was made to stand up and you were asked is that the man?—He had his head down. That is why I didn't recognise him. I had to ask for the man to stand up.

Do you swear that?—Yes, sir.

I put it to you that when you were describing this man to the police on the Monday following this crime, the man who was on the dark side with a pale face, you were describing not this man but some other man entirely?—No, sir.

You gave your description to the police on the Monday which would be 21 October. That is right, is it not?—Yes.

When you gave that description to the police, was there a man in custody?—No, sir.

Or detained?—No, sir. Not that I know of.

How d'you know?—Not that I know of.

I don't want you to take this question in the wrong sense, because it's not meant in that way. Did anybody give you any money in a place near the police station?—No, sir.

Please don't think I'm suggesting you were in any way induced by money to give wrong evidence. I'm not suggesting that.—No, sir. I wouldn't do that.

No, I'm sure you wouldn't.—No, sir. It is too serious.

Did you go and have something to drink in licensed premises?—I had a pint of beer.

Near the police station?—Yes, sir.

Were police officers present?—There was one present.

Who was that?—I couldn't tell you which one it was, sir. It was the officer that was taking me back home in the car.

Did you have a drink together?—We had a drink, yes. I paid for the drinks.

Please don't think I'm making any wrong suggestions

against you, Mr MacDonald. Did you know that at that time there was a man who was detained?—No, sir.

And that the description which you had given of a man on the dark side with a pale face fitted the man who was then detained? Did you know that?—No, sir. It's the first I've heard of it.

Re-examined by MR NIELD: . . .

You were asked if you had given the police a statement? Is that your signature? [*Document handed*]—Yes, sir. That is my signature.

In the course of that statement covering these particular points that have been raised, did you say this: 'At about 11 am Saturday, 19 October 1946, I purchased a "house-clearing" at 116 North Road, Longsight. The occupier Mr Rawlinson was in the boot and shoe repairing line of business and amongst the goods I purchased were a quantity of boot and shoe making tools and accessories. Among these latter articles was a leather dresser's hammer and the one you've shown to me is definitely the one I got from Mr Rawlinson. The hammer and other articles were removed by me to my shop premises, 3 Downing Street, Manchester, and placed on sale at about 3 pm on the same day, 19 October 1946, the hammer being placed in the window. Between 5 and 6 pm that evening a customer came into the shop and, pointing to the leather dresser's hammer in the window, asked the price of it. I told him three shillings and sixpence and pointed out to him that it was a special leather dresser's hammer. He told me that that was quite all right because he only wanted it for general purposes. I then wrapped the hammer up in a piece of brown crepe paper from a roll in my shop which I keep for that purpose and I can definitely identify the brown paper you've shown to me as that I wrapped the hammer in before passing it to the customer. The man gave me a half-crown and a shilling in payment. I produce a piece of brown crepe paper from the same roll as that which I wrapped the hammer. The description of the man who bought the hammer is: 28 to 32 years, five foot seven or eight in height, medium build, very pale face, thin features, clean-shaven, quiet spoken, no hat, white soft collar and shirt, dark tie, dark suit and a dark fawn cotton raincoat. He was of clean and respectable appearance. After making the purchase, the man put the hammer in his raincoat pocket and after leaving my shop turned down the road towards the city.' . . .

On the 27th October you attended a parade?—Yes, sir.

Can you say how many men there were upon that parade? —I should say about fourteen. Something like that. I never counted them.

Did you look at these men with care?—Yes, sir.

Had you any doubt in selecting which one it was that bought the hammer?—No, sir. I went straight to him.

Let us face the situation. You've been asked about pints of beer and so on. Do you know what the charge is against this man?—Yes.

Is it he or no?—Yes. That is the man I sold the hammer to.

THE PRISONER: You're a liar.

MRS AGNES HALL ROWLAND, *of 65 Bridge Street, New Mills, Derbyshire [where Rowland was born in 1908], examined by* MR WINGATE-SAUL, *said that she was the wife of Isaac Rowland and the mother of the accused who was 38 years old. She saw her son at 65 Bridge Street on 19 October at half-past seven pm. That was the first time she had seen him that day. He stayed at their home until twenty minutes past nine the same evening. He said that he was going to Manchester by bus. He left at about twenty past nine. When he arrived home he was wearing a dark blue suit and brown shoes and a brown striped collar—shirt with collar to match. He had no coat with him. He changed his underclothes but not his suit. He had the same suit on when he left. He was wearing a pale blue shirt with a soft collar when he left and he took with him two khaki shirts and a pair of overalls wrapped up in light brown paper. She said that he had the habit of sending his laundry home to her to wash and she used to send it after she had washed it back to him in Manchester. She said that on 17 October she sent to him a shirt and pants and vest and socks which she had washed in a parcel.*

In cross-examination by MR BURKE *she said that she washed the collar and tie which he took off and that it was a separate brown-striped collar and a brown-striped shirt. She said that she had never seen her son wearing a white soft collar and shirt. The suit that he was wearing when he came home and when he left home was his demob suit and that he had no* macintosh or brown paper parcel when he arrived at the house. She said that his jacket was put over a chair and while it was there it was knocked over by her and fell on the ground, that she picked it up and threw it over the back of the chair. She said that when it dropped on the ground she heard no thud as you would have expected if a heavy thing were dropped. It was just the right weight for a man's coat.

In re-examination by MR NIELD she said that the bus which her son went to catch was the half-past nine bus from New Mills. In order to go to Manchester you have to change at Stockport if you take that bus. Finally she said that in order to reach her home at half-past seven he would have had to have caught the half-past six bus at Lower Moseley Street.

WILLIAM GRAHAM GALLIMORE, detective-sergeant in the Manchester City Police, examined by MR NIELD, said that on 2 November he took a bus from New Mills to Stockport and from Stockport to Manchester in order to time and test the journey. He said that he had boarded the bus at New Mills at 9.30 pm and got off at Mersey Square, Stockport, at one minute to ten. He then boarded another bus opposite the Touchstone Inn which left at 10.3 pm. He got off the bus at the Piccadilly bus station, Manchester, and it was then 10.20 pm. He walked from the bus station to the Queen's Café near Deansgate and he arrived at the café at 10.30 pm.

In cross-examination by MR BURKE he said that he did not know the Wellington Hotel, Mersey Square, Stockport. He said that he didn't have a drink when he changed buses at Stockport but that he would have had time to have one or possibly two and still catch the bus which arrived in Manchester at 10.30 pm. He said that that would have meant that he arrived at the Queen's Café at 10.35 pm. He said that he had four minutes in which to catch the bus at Stockport for Manchester. He said that from his enquiries and experience you could get to Manchester from Stockport in fifteen minutes at that time of night.

JACK BASKEYFIELD of 23 Langdale Road, Heaton Chapel, examined by MR NIELD, said that he was a bus driver employed by the North Western Road Car Company Limited and that on 19 October he was the driver of bus No 981 which passed *through New Mills on its way to Stockport. He said that they left New Mills at 9.30 pm and that the ordinary running time made them reach Stockport at nine minutes past ten. He said that he sometimes did the journey and arrived before the scheduled time and that sometimes they got in on the hour, that is nine minutes before time, and sometimes they got in at five minutes past. He said that this depended on the traffic. He could not say exactly at what time he arrived at Stockport on the occasion in question.*

LAWRENCE HOLLINGSWORTH, of 5 Broad Street, Hulme, Manchester, examined by MR NIELD, said that he was an omnibus driver employed by the Manchester Corporation and that for the last year he had been driving on the No 20 route which went via Stockport to Manchester. He said that on 19 October his bus left Stockport at 10.5 pm and that he reached Piccadilly, Manchester, at approximately 10.25 pm.

RITA LEACH, of 25 Higher Chatham Street, Chorlton-on-Medlock, examined by MR WINGATE-SAUL, said that on 19 October between nine and a quarter past she was coming from the GPO in Manchester and going towards Piccadilly. She said that a lady came and asked her the way to Deansgate and that she walked a little way with her. She said that she walked down King Street towards Deansgate. She said that she left her at the bottom of King Street and Corporation Street. She said that the lady went straight across the road down, she thought, St Anne's Street, the continuation of King Street. She said that that was in the direction of Deansgate. She said that she left her at about quarter or twenty past nine. She looked at the hat and coat which had been removed from Olive Balchin's body and identified both of them as having been worn by her when she saw her. Then she was shown a photograph of Olive Balchin after she was dead and after her face had been washed. She said that that was the woman whom she saw.

In cross-examination by MR BURKE, she said that she had no doubt that Olive Balchin was wearing a hat when she saw her.

MRS ELIZABETH COPLEY, of 194 Heald Grove, Rusholme, Manchester, examined by MR NIELD, said that she was employed as a waitress at the Queen's Café which is in Queen Street, just opposite Deansgate, and was so employed on 19

*October last. She said that she was working there between
10 and 11 pm on that evening.*

MR NIELD: Did you notice certain persons come into your
café?—Yes, sir.

Who were they?—The young girl—Olive—I cannot just
pronounce that name.

Men or women first and how many?—Two women. One
was an elderly woman.

One elderly and one younger woman?—Yes. And the
young man came in.

Did the man come in after the two women or with them?
—He came in with them but he was the last to come down
the stairs.

Now, with regard to the younger of these two women.
Would you look at Exhibit 3, which is a coat, and tell my
lord and the jury whether that was the coat worn by the
younger woman?—Yes, this is the coat.

[*That was the coat shown in the photograph on p. 33*]

Who came in at about half-past ten?—Yes.

Look at Exhibit 2, the photograph at the bottom.—Yes.
This is the girl.

Is that the girl?—Yes, definitely.

MR JUSTICE SELLERS: About what time is this?—It would
be about half-past ten. They went out just before eleven.

MR NIELD: What did you say?—They came in at half-past
ten and went out just before eleven.

MR JUSTICE SELLERS: All three of them?—Yes.

MR NIELD: Looking round this court, do you see the man
who was with these two women? Look carefully everywhere.
—Yes, sir. That is the gentleman.

MR JUSTICE SELLERS: The man between the two police
officers?—Yes, sir.

MR NIELD: Did you notice anything about his hair at the
time as compared with it now?—It had a bit more grease on
it. That is all. It was plastered down.

Was he carrying anything at the time he came into your
café?—It was a small parcel. A brown one.

Was it a thick parcel or a thin parcel?—No, it was only a
thin parcel. It was not thick.

About what length would you say the thin parcel was?—It
would be about a foot.

How was it wrapped?—Well, I never really noticed that.

You said something about brown?—It was brown paper—it was in brown paper . . .

You say they all left together about eleven o'clock?—It may be before eleven because our clock's a bit fast. We generally have fifteen minutes.

Did you see where he placed the thin parcel about a foot in length?—Yes. It was under the table near his chair.

Did he take that out with him or not?—He took it out with him certainly.

On 27 October did you go to a police station and attend an identification parade?—Yes.

Could you say approximately how many men were lined up for you?—I never counted them.

There were several?—There were a lot more than seven.

No, I said several.—Yes, several.

Did you point to someone in the line?—Yes, sir.

Who was he?—He was that young man.

This young man?—Yes.

Mrs Copley, you realise the gravity of this matter, do you not?—Yes.

I want you to tell my lord and the jury quite carefully and clearly, is there any doubt in your mind about it?—No, sir.

Cross-examined by MR BURKE:

There is no doubt in your mind now?—No.

When you attended the identification parade you pointed to this man?—Yes.

You were pointing to the man whom you thought had been in the café and you had described with these two women?—It was the man that came into the café.

Did you say this? 'That looks like the man but I'm not sure.'—I did at the time. Yes, sir. But his hair was all over his face. He was different when I said I see him on the Saturday night.

That is what you said at the identification parade?—Yes, I did, sir.

MR JUSTICE SELLERS: How d'you mean his hair was—not brushed?—No, it looked as though it had been washed and it had all fallen, with no grease on it or anything and he didn't look as smart.

MR BURKE: Pardon?—It did not look as smart.

Are you sure of the time when you first saw these three people in this café—Yes.

So it was 10.30 pm, was it not?—Yes, sir.

Are you sure of this?—Yes, sir. Positive.

Are you sure of the time when they left?—Yes, sir.

Was that at eleven o'clock?—Eleven by the clock, yes.

Had you ever seen any of these three people before?—Well, I had seen the old lady before.

Is she a lady whom you describe as having a Welsh accent?—No, she was not Welsh.

What?—She was not Welsh. She was more Irish, I should imagine. She was a very old woman. She was well over sixty.

MR JUSTICE SELLERS: You should not over-emphasise the age.—She might have been going on seventy, sir.

MR BURKE: How many times did you see her before?—Once before.

With regard to the man and the younger woman. Had you ever, so far as you know, seen either of them before?—Yes, I had seen that young man before.

Many times? . . .—About twice.

Had you ever seen the younger woman before?—Never in my life.

How old did she look?—I should say she was about my age. About thirty-eight.

You kept on referring to her a few minutes ago as a young girl?—She looked young.

MR JUSTICE SELLERS: That was your view of it?—Yes.

MR BURKE: Did you notice whether her hair was going grey or not?—No. I noticed it was tinted. She was a bit sandy, you know.

MR JUSTICE SELLERS: A bit what?—A bit sandy. She'd had it touched up auburn.

Auburn?—Yes.

MR BURKE: Was she wearing a hat?—Not at the time.

Are you sure of that?—I didn't see her have it on. She had it at the side of her.

She had it at the side of her?—Yes. On the chair.

Did you see it?—Yes, but she had not got it on.

Have you ever said that before?—No, sir.

Did you say at the police court that you never saw a hat

either on her head or anywhere else?—Oh no, sir. I said I had not seen her with a hat but she had it with her.

Did you say at the police court that she may have had it in her hand but I did not see it. Did you say that?—I don't think I said that.

D'you say you never said it?—I do not know. I will not say that.

When did you suddenly remember that you saw a hat on the chair?—Well, it came back to me as things do sometimes.

When did it come back to you?—I cannot just think.

Was it after the police court proceedings that it suddenly came back to you that you had seen a hat on the chair?—I think it may have been . . .

What was there about these people that specially attracted your attention?—Well, just at the time we was very slack. We had only had half-a-dozen in at that time of the night.

Saturday night?—Yes, certainly. We had a very slack time about that time of night.

What was there about them that specially attracted your attention?—Was it because there were so few people there? —Yes.

Was that the only reason?—The gentleman was a bit annoyed. What it was over I don't know.

A bit annoyed?—Yes. He was not speaking much to them.

This was on 19 October?—Yes.

When were you first asked to remember by the police this matter of seeing these people in the café?—Well, I came on my own.

Pardon?—I came on my own.

To the police?—Yes.

When was that?—I cannot just think about the dates.

How long afterwards about?—I cannot think. About two or three days afterwards.

Had you read the description in the newspapers?—No, sir.

Of the man who was wanted in connection with this crime?—No, I've never read the paper. Never.

You have not?—I never read the paper.

You have not?—No, I never bother much.

What was it caused you to go to the police with this information?—Well, I was asked to assist them as much as I could when they came round.

So you did not go to the police of your own accord? The police came to you, did they, and asked if you could assist them?—Well, they came to see if they'd been in the café and I said Yes.

If who had been in the café—The two people and the gentleman.

Did they mention three people?—They didn't mention it because they didn't know.

What description did the police officers give you?—They gave me none.

Is that all the police officers said to you?—Yes.

Have you seen three people in your café?—They came to ask me if I'd seen anybody who'd looked strange in the café.

That looked strange?—Yes. Strange people. So I just told them.

What did you mean by people who looked strange?—How d'you mean?

You say the police officers, whoever they were, asked you if you'd seen anybody who looked strange in the café?—Yes, well we do have a lot of strangers in.

You mean who look like strangers. Is that what you understood the police meant?—Yes.

He was not a stranger, was he, if he'd been there twice before?—The young girl was a stranger.

She was a stranger? What else did the police ask you when they came?—They asked me nothing else.

Did you describe the man to the police?—Yes.

Did you say he was a dark man?—I said he had dark hair.

You said he had dark hair?—Yes, but a fresh complexion.

He hasn't got dark hair, has he?—He had at the time but he'd greased it. Grease makes your hair look black.

Grease doesn't make that kind of hair look black.—Yes it did at the time, definitely.

Did you say his hair looked black?—I did not say very black. I said black.

Did you describe to the police officers how he was dressed? —Yes, I did.

What did you have to say about that?—I just said he had a dark suit on.

Anything else?—No, nothing in particular.

Had you noticed anything else about his dress?—No, I don't think I did.

Did you notice whether he was wearing a hat?—He did not wear a hat.

Did you see him wearing a mackintosh?—I didn't see a mackintosh.

This was a thin parcel?—Yes, sir.

And might have contained that hammer?—It might have done, yes.

Not the sort of parcel which might have contained two shirts and some socks and an overall, was it?—No, nothing like that.

How long did it take you to pick him out at the identification parade?—Well, I went down three times to make sure. I didn't want to pick the wrong person out.

How long did it take?—About five minutes maybe. It may be ten. I didn't notice the time.

It may be ten?—It may be ten.

To pick out a man you'd seen three times before?—I didn't know I'd seen him three times before until after when I remembered when I first worked there. That night I was on I had only come on at nine o'clock because of the waitress there.

You know now?—The same one. Yes.

You know now that you had seen him three times before the identification parade?—Twice before that time.

There was the time when according to you he was there with the elderly woman and the younger woman?—Yes.

I understood you to say that you'd seen him twice before that?—Yes, sir.

So that you'd seen him three times before the identification parade?—Well, yes. That is right.

It must be so?—That is right, yes.

And it took five minutes to pick him out?—Well, I had to have a good look, didn't I?

You wanted to make sure?—Certainly I did.

Is that why you took such a long time?—It may be, yes.

You found it difficult?—No.

You wanted to be sure?—Yes.

Then when you'd picked him out, although you'd taken all that trouble in order to make sure, you said, 'That looks like the man but I'm not sure,' didn't you?—Yes, I think I did say that, sir.

You looked at the clock, didn't you, when they left the premises at eleven o'clock?—Yes. I always do.

That is why you've got eleven o'clock fixed in your mind? —I generally look at the clock because sometimes we have customers coming in and sometimes they want to know if a person comes in what time they go out and I generally tell them.

Did you look at the clock when they came in?—Not just when they came in. Previous to that I looked at it.

These people you are speaking about who were in the café that night came in at 10.30?—Yes, sir.

And left as near as anything on the stroke of eleven?—Yes.

Re-examined by MR NIELD:

You were asked about what you said in the court below about identification. Did you there say, 'When I attended the identification parade I pointed to the prisoner and said "that looked like the man but I was not sure" '?—Yes, I think I did say that.

Did you go on to say at the police court, 'I'm sure this morning that it is the prisoner. His hair was untidy at the identification parade'?—Yes, it was, sir. Very.

It was greased then?—It was well greased when I see him. It was greased in the café?—Yes.

MR JUSTICE SELLERS: You say you knew the elderly woman who was there?—Yes. She had been in the café once before when I worked regularly there, but I had been left three months until the Saturday I was on.

You had seen that lady before?—Yes. At a time when I was on. When I was a waitress.

NORMAN MERCER, *licensee of the Dog & Partridge Inn, at 298 Deansgate, Manchester, examined by* MR NIELD, *said that on the evening of 19 October he was in Deansgate at twelve midnight. He said that he was taking the dog for a run. He said that he was on the left hand side of the road in Deansgate, the same side as Cumberland Street, and that when he came to the corner of Cumberland Street he saw two people, one man and a woman.*

MR NIELD: I want you to tell us, if you know, living in this part, if you are walking along Deansgate and get to the corner of Cumberland Street, is it a right angle like that or has the corner a curve in it? Is it cut off?—No, it is a right angle. You can see it as you are coming up.

MR JUSTICE SELLERS: Is what a right angle?

MR NIELD: I wondered if the wall of Cumberland Street went at right angles to Deansgate or whether there was a space there. Whether it was cut off. In other words, I was wondering if it was cut away.

MR JUSTICE SELLERS: Is it a square corner or is it cut away? —No, you can see the full corner as you are coming along Deansgate.

It's a square corner?—Yes.

MR NIELD: On that corner you saw a man and a woman, you say?—Yes.

What was the woman's position?—She was stood with her back against the wall facing me. I could see her full face as I came up Deansgate.

Where was the man?—I could see the full profile of the man as I came up Deansgate. He was stood sideways.

Towards her?—Yes.

And what was the position? What were they doing or engaged in?—They were in a quarrel. Arguing.

Did you pay any particular attention to them?—Yes, because they were arguing at that time of the night. You do not always see anybody just about there.

I want you, if you will, to look at Exhibit 3. Did you notice the sort of coat worn by the woman who was standing with her back to the wall in the corner?—Yes.

Would you look at that coat and see if it is anything like it?—Yes. I should say it was the same coat.

I want you to tell the jury. Did you go to the Platt Lane Police Station mortuary on 20 October? That is the next day?—Yes.

In the presence of Inspector Stainton did you see the body of a woman?—Yes.

Did you recognise her?—Yes.

As whom?—As the same woman as I'd seen the night before.

I want you to tell us, Mr Mercer. Would you look round

the court and say whether you see the man who was in argument or a quarrel with that woman?—Yes. Stood there.

Between the two police officers?—Yes.

You appreciate the gravity of this matter, do you not, Mr Mercer?—Yes.

Have you any doubt about that?—No doubt whatsoever.

Now, that is at midnight. A quarrel and an argument. Did you proceed with your walk with the dog?—Yes.

Did you come back again to this same corner shortly afterwards?—Yes.

About how long afterwards?—Half an hour.

Were either of those two persons then to be seen?—No.

On 4 November did you attend an identification parade at the Manchester prison?—Yes.

Did you then see a number of men standing in the line? —Yes.

Did you then pick out the man whom you had seen at midnight on 19 October in argument with this woman?— Yes.

Is this the man?—The same one.

Cross-examined by MR BURKE:

The identification parade was on 4 November, was it not? —Yes.

Was it held at His Majesty's prison, Strangeways?—Yes.

Were prison officers in charge at the time?—Yes.

On 4 November. This was sixteen days, was it not, after the night when you saw this man and woman quarrelling in Deansgate?—Yes.

How long before you attended the identity parade was it when you were interviewed about this matter by the police? —I would say a week.

Nine or ten days after 19 October?—Yes.

How did you come to be interviewed by the police? Did they come to see you or did you come to see them?—No. Some people came to my place and said there's been a murder up Deansgate. I said, 'Who was it?' and they told me it was a woman. I said I'd seen a couple at twelve o'clock. I wondered if it could be the same woman and I gave a description of the woman. He said it was the same woman as I'd given a description to, so I phoned the police and told them.

When was that?—The Sunday the body was found.

Did you telephone the police on that Sunday?—The Sunday that the body was found? Yes.

Did you describe the man to the police?—The night I saw the man?

On the 20th?—Yes. He was of proportionate build and had a dark suit on and appeared to have dark hair on the night I see him.

When you attended this identification parade at the prison there were a number of men lined up in a row, were there not?—Yes.

Did you go up and down that line?—Yes.

Repeatedly?—No.

Without picking anybody out?—No, I just walked up twice. That is all.

Did it take you four or five minutes?—Yes.

And then did you request to see the men in profile?—Yes.

To whom did you address that request?—The inspector on parade.

What did you say?—I said, 'Could you give me the profile of the men that is on parade now?' And he did so.

Did you close up to these men and look at them very closely?—No.

When you asked for a profile view, did you ask that the men be requested to turn to their right?—Yes.

Why to the right? Was there any special reason?—Because that is the way I had seen the prisoner as I came up Deansgate.

Then, when they were all turning with their faces to the right, you approached them from the right of the line, did you not?—No. I was looking right at the front of the prisoner when I picked him out.

It is not unusual, is it, for people to quarrel together at street corners late on a Saturday night?—No, I had not seen it before and I take the dog out regular.

Did you slacken your pace as you got to those people in order that you might observe them better?—I couldn't slacken it much more. I would have stopped walking if I had done.

Do you know that this man Rowland has a scar on the back of his ear here?—No. I do not.

Is that what you were looking for when you asked that

F

they should give you a profile view?—No. I didn't know he had a scar.

Had anybody told you before that identification parade took place?—Nobody.

Whether this man had a scar behind his ear?—No.

You had seen the photographs, had you not?—Of the prisoner? No. I had seen no photographs of the prisoner.

Some photographs, I said?—No. I had seen no photographs.

Before this identification parade, you had seen some photographs?—Just to identify him, yes.

To identify him? What does that mean?—I thought you said I had seen photographs of the prisoner?

No. I first of all asked whether you had seen some photographs?—Yes.

You replied yes to identify him. What does that mean?—Yes. Well, I had seen some photographs.

Where had you seen them?—At Bootle Street.

At Bootle Street Police Station?—Yes.

How many had you seen?—I don't know. I've seen quite a few. How many I just don't know.

Had you seen one of Rowland?—No.

Why did you say a moment ago that you'd seen some photographs in order to identify him?—I thought you said had I seen a photograph of the prisoner? Had they actually shown him to me?

How many photographs had you seen?—I'd seen a few.

At the time this man was in custody?—No. He'd not been picked up then. I went to see the photographs on the same Sunday as I went to see the body.

Did you pick Rowland's photograph out then?—No.

Are you sure it was not there?—I am positive that it was not there. I have never seen it.

Had you seen a photograph of Rowland?—I had seen no photograph of Rowland.

Before you went to this identification parade?—I had seen none whatever.

With regard to the woman. I understand you to say when you went to see the woman's body at the mortuary on 20 October you recognised her?—Yes.

She was in a sorry state, was she not?—Yes.

Did you say in the police court this: 'Her features were similar to those of the woman whom I saw the previous night'?—That is right.

Would you like to be sure it was the same woman?—I am positive it was the same woman.

You were not positive at the police court, were you?—I was as positive then as when I saw the woman.

When you used these words 'that her features were similar to those of the woman whom I saw the previous night'?—I'm positive it was the woman I had seen on the Saturday night.

Did you mean in the police court those words I have quoted?—I meant it was the same woman.

There was a resemblance?—No, I didn't mention the word 'resemblance'. I didn't say 'resemblance' whatsoever.

Did you see this woman wearing a hat?—No.

Would you say she was not wearing a hat?—She could have been but it must have been on the back of her head. I couldn't say she was not. It might have been a small hat on the back of her head?—Yes.

Are you sure of this? That facing her from the front no hat was visible to you?—No.

Did you notice the colour of her hair?—Yes, it was a brownish colour.

A light brown or a dark brown?—No. A lightish brown.

The man in the dock has light hair, has he not?—Yes.

It looked dark to you?—Yes. It could have been well-greased, as I told the inspector on the phone.

Well-greased?—I said it appeared dark to me, but it could have been well-greased to give a darker appearance.

When you were giving your description to the police on the telephone, did you say then that his hair seemed dark but might have been well-greased?—Not on the telephone. When the police came down to interview me.

Was that shortly after the telephone conversation?—Yes.

Did you put that in writing?—I didn't put nothing in writing. They wrote it down for me and I signed it.

You describe the man as thirty to thirty-five years. Is that right?—Yes.

Five foot seven, proportionate build, full round face, clean-shaven?—Yes.

Dark hair?—Yes.

Dressed in a blue suit?—Yes.

He was of clean and tidy appearance?—Yes.

You never mentioned a word about his hair being greased, did you?—Not in writing, no.

CHARLES UTTLEY, *inspector in the Manchester City Police, examined by* MR WINGATE-SAUL, *said that on Sunday, 27 October, he was in charge of an identification parade held at Bootle Street Police Station at about 3 o'clock in the afternoon. He said that Rowland was put up for identification with ten other men who were similar in height and dress to the prisoner. He said that Rowland was told by him to choose his position in the line and he chose to stand between Nos 3 and 4. He asked him whether he had any objection to make to any other men in the parade and he said that he had not.*

Elizabeth Copley was first brought on to the parade to see if she could identify anyone. He said that before she was brought on to the parade she had had no opportunity of seeing any of the men who formed the parade. He said that she came on to the parade and walked from the left, that she passed seven men and hesitated in front of the prisoner and then walked to the extreme end of the line. She then returned, stopped in front of the prisoner, placed her right hand on his shoulder and said, 'I'm not certain, but I think this is him'. She was then taken to another room and had no opportunity of speaking to Mr MacDonald who came next on to the parade.

Before MacDonald came on to the parade the witness asked the prisoner if he wished to change his place in the parade and he said that he did not. When MacDonald came on to the parade he looked at the men assembled, went straight to the accused and laid his hand on his shoulder. The witness said that he then asked Rowland if he had any complaints to make as to the way in which the parade was conducted and he said that he had not.

In cross-examination by MR BURKE *the witness said that Mrs Copley did not walk to and fro once or twice. He said that the parade took two minutes, not five or ten minutes.*

RICHARD MCLEOD, *inspector in the Manchester City Police, examined by* MR WINGATE-SAUL, *said that on 4 November 1946 he was in charge of an identification parade at Strange-*

*ways Prison, at half past three pm. He said that the prisoner
was put up for identification with eight other men. He said
that the other men were all of similar build and colouring
and that their general appearance was very similar to his. He
said that Rowland was asked if he had any objection to any
of the men and he said that he had not. Rowland was allowed
to choose his own position in the line and took up his position between Nos 5 and 6. He said that Mr Hinchcliffe, Rowland's solicitor, was present. He said that Mercer came on to
the parade to see if he could identify anyone. He said that he
examined the line all the way along the line as they were
standing drawn up facing towards the front. He then turned
away from the line and approached the witness and asked to
see the line side-face. The witness said he asked the parade
to turn half-right and they did so. Mercer then again examined the line and he went up and touched Rowland and
walked off the parade. He said that from the time when
Mercer came on to the parade to the time that he touched the
prisoner it was about a minute and a half to two minutes.
He asked the prisoner if he had any objection to the identification parade after it was over and the prisoner replied: 'I
am satisfied'. He said that Mercer had no opportunity of seeing the prisoner or any of the other men who were on the
parade that day before the parade.*

In cross-examination by MR BURKE *the witness said that the
parade did not take as long as four to five minutes. He said
that he had timed it by his watch but that he did not make
a note of the time and was relying on his memory.*

SECOND DAY *Friday, 13 December 1946*

MRS AGNES HALL ROWLAND, *recalled at the request of* MR
BURKE, *for further cross-examination said that her son had
never used grease on his hair in his life, only water. She said
that in November 1945 he was in the Army and he came
home on leave. She said that she bought him a bottle of
brilliantine and that when she presented it to him he said
that he did not want it and that the boys would call him a
'cissy'. She said that she gave the bottle of brilliantine to his
brother who used it.*

Re-examined by MR NIELD, *she said that when Rowland put water on his hair it looked darker at the front. It wasn't very wet. The effect was to make his hair slightly darker but not much and just at the front.*

WALTER JOHN HARRIS, *of 36 Hyde Road, Ardwick, Manchester, examined by* MR NIELD, *said that he kept a hotel at 36 Hyde Road. He remembered the night of Sunday, 20 October, and identified Rowland as coming to his hotel for accommodation that night. He said that he came between 10.30 and 11 pm. He said that he had a faint recollection that Rowland said that he had come from Bolton and that he had come to Manchester for a job and that he was starting work on the Monday in Great Jackson Street, Hulme. He said that Rowland showed him a labour card and said that he was going for the job, a block of flats or something they are building. He produced the register which Rowland signed in his own name. He said that he was leaving on the 21st and that he was wearing a blue-striped suit, blue-striped shirt and brown shoes and that he did not see him carrying any coat. He said that when they were in the dining-room there was a raincoat hanging over a chair and that as he was the only person present he presumed that it was his. The witness said that Rowland left at approximately 10 am on 21 October and said that he was going for his employment as a joiner and that he would be back as soon as he had settled his business. He came back at about twelve. Then he had a meal and finally left.*

Cross-examined by MR BURKE, *he said that Rowland made no attempt to conceal his identity.*

Re-examined by MR NIELD, *he said that Rowland had stated that he was going to Seddon Limited, Hulme, for the job and that he wrote that name in the visitors' book by his own name.*

THOMAS REID, *of the Salvation Army Hostel, 26 Clifford Street, Chorlton-upon-Medlock, examined by* MR WINGATE-SAUL, *said that he was a captain in the Salvation Army and that on 21 October Rowland came to the Salvation Army Hostel of which he was in charge between 10.15 and 10.30 am. He said that his hair appeared dark, well-greased, with hair cream on it and brushed back. He said that he asked for a cubicle but he was unable to fix him up with one as he had*

*not one available but that he could give him a bed in a
dormitory. He said that he stayed at the hostel for four days,
that is from the 21st to the 24th inclusive, and he issued him
with a ticket for each night. The tickets were issued separ-
ately each day. The tickets found on Rowland were produced
to the witness who identified them. He said that when he
came on the 21st he was in a dark suit. Rowland said to the
witness that on the previous night he had stayed at the Sinclair Hotel but that he (the witness) had no idea where that
was. On 22 October Rowland asked if he could leave a small
parcel at the hostel, a small brown paper parcel. He identified the paper in which the parcel came as the paper in which
Mrs Rowland had sent the laundry to him. He said that
Rowland left the hostel on Friday, the 25th, and did not
return after that.*

Cross-examined by MR BURKE, *he said that Rowland made
no attempt to conceal his identity. He said that Rowland had
no mackintosh with him.*

DETECTIVE CONSTABLE DOUGLAS NIMMO, *detective-constable
in the Manchester City Police, examined by* MR NIELD, *said
that on Saturday, 26 October, at about 11 pm with Detective
Sergeant Blakemore he called at the Services' Transit Dormitory at Long Millgate. He saw the accused in bed apparently
asleep. He said that he woke him and told him to get dressed
as he wanted to see him. He said that Rowland sat up in bed
and, when he saw him, said, 'You don't want me for murdering that fucking woman, do you?' He said that he then
cautioned him and said that Inspector Stainton wanted to
see him at Police Headquarters. He said that Rowland got
up and dressed and while he was dressing said, 'Is it about
that coat?'*

*He said that he then took him to Police Headquarters
where he was interviewed by Detective Inspector Stainton
and that he was present throughout that interview. In the
course of the interview he said that Rowland asked if he
could make a statement and that he was told that he could
if he wanted to. He said that he heard everything that
was said during the interview and made a note of it. He
said that they arrived at the Police Headquarters at about
11.30 pm and that he heard Inspector Stainton question
the accused. Inspector Stainton said, 'I am investigating the*

*death of a woman named Olive Balchin which took place
on the site of a bombed building in Deansgate, Manchester,
between 11 pm on the 19th and 11 am on the 20th October.
You answer the description of a man seen in the company
of the dead woman late on the Saturday night, the 19th.
Do you care to give me an account of your movements on
Saturday, the 19th, and Sunday, the 20th?'* He said that the
accused replied, *'I am admitting nothing because it is only
a fool's game to do that. I can account for where I was. I was
at home at New Mills when she was murdered. I did not
come back to Manchester that night.'*

He was then asked by Inspector Stainton, *'Do you care to
tell me where you stayed on that Saturday night, the 19th?'*
and Rowland said, *'Have you seen my mother?'* and Inspector Stainton told him that he had not. The witness then said
that Rowland said, *'Well, I did come back to Manchester. I
got a lift in a car and then went to a pub for a drink. I didn't
go into Deansgate. I stayed in the Ardwick district and had a
bit of supper and stayed at Grafton House in Hyde Road. I
didn't get in until after one o'clock.'*

The inspector then said to him, *'It will be necessary for
me to make enquiries at Grafton House to prove your statements'*, and Rowland then said, *'Well, I didn't stay there. I
stayed at 36 Hyde Road and I only stayed there one night.'*
Inspector Stainton said, *'Do you know Olive Balchin?'* and
Rowland replied, *'Yes, I've known her for about eight weeks.
I used to call her "Lil". I made sure that she did not know
my name. Have you a photo of her?'* Inspector Stainton then
said, *'I've only got a photo of her after she was dead. It isn't
pleasant to look upon. I don't propose to show it to you. She's
been badly knocked about and it would be difficult to identify her.'* Rowland then said, *'Things like that don't happen
to decent women and whoever did it didn't do it without a
cause. You can't see what you've done in the dark. Let me
see it and I will tell you if it is the same woman'*.

The witness said that Rowland was then shown a photograph of the clothing of the deceased but that the clothing
was being worn by another woman. He said that Rowland,
on being shown the photograph, said *'That's her coat and
hat but it's not the woman.'* He was then shown two further
photographs showing Olive Balchin after she was dead, the*

*one with her face washed and the other with her face
touched up on the negative. Having seen those he said, 'Yes,
that's her but I've got a fighting chance and I'm going to
hang on to it. I've got an uncontrollable temper but that's
not evidence, is it? I'm sure I didn't do that. It's possible the
hammer was got to do a job with. I was not going to do a job
that night. The fact that I went home proved that, unless you
think I could the job when I came back. I'm not admitting
anything. I came back on the 9.30 bus and got off at Ardwick.
I was never near that place on Saturday night. I know where
it is because I walked past it on Tuesday but I didn't go on
the site.' Inspector Stainton then asked him if he was wearing a raincoat on Saturday, the 19th, and he said that he was
wearing the suit which he had on. He said, 'I had a mac I
borrowed from a man I only know as "Slim". I have given
it back to him.' He then produced a document issued by a
Dr Parkinson and said, 'I might as well show you this. You
will find it. I had a pride in my body. It was a blow to find I
had VD. I wanted to know where I got it. If I had been sure
it was her I would have strangled her. I did think it was her.
It's hard to say it was her now. Has she VD? If she gave it to
me, she deserves all she got.' He was then told that he would
be detained and put up for identification and he asked to
make a statement and he made one and it was taken down.
The witness read out the statement (which was Exhibit
34) which went as follows:*

I, Walter Graham Rowland, have been told by Detective Inspector Stainton that I am not obliged to say
anything unless I wish to do so, but that whatever I do
say will be taken down in writing and may be given in
evidence.

*The witness said that Rowland signed that part of the
statement and that the statement went on:*

I first met Olive Balchin in Lockhart's Café near
Victoria Station about seven or eight weeks ago. Since
then I've met her on three or four occasions. I have had
intercourse with her twice, once on Baxendale's blitzed
building site and the other time in a doorway in a side
street. Shortly after I had intercourse with her I suspected

that I had contracted venereal disease . . . I was convinced that I had got venereal disease.

On Friday night, 18 October, I went to Littlewoods café in Piccadilly and I saw Olive Balchin there. I knew her as 'Lil'. I bought her cakes and tea. It was in my mind to try to find out whether she had this complaint without letting her know. I left there at about quarter or half-past nine with Lil and I left her at the bottom of the stairs and went down towards London Road station for a drink in The Feathers. Later I went to the NAAFI and stayed there. Before I left her I said I would see her the following night. On Saturday morning I went up to Old Trafford, Trafford Park, to do some business. I met a girl named Edith I know. We went on a tram to a café in Salford, not far from the Ship Hotel. We had a cup of tea. She had no money and I had no money. I left her. I told her I was going to the Post Office but I went to meet some of the boys to get some money.

I met the boys at Liston's Bar and had a few drinks with them. We went to Yates and had a few more. At 3 o'clock I left them and went back to the café where I saw Edith. She started creating, so I left her and came down town again and I knocked about town and had a wash. I went to the Post Office for a parcel I was expecting but it wasn't there so I decided to go home for it.

I got a bus at Lower Moseley Street and went to New Mills where I arrived at about quarter past eight. I went to my mother's house. I changed my things there and put on all clean stuff. Then I came back on the bus to Stockport, arriving there at about ten o'clock. I had a few drinks in the bottom Wellington. I took a bus to Manchester and got off at Ardwick. I went up Brunswick Street and had some supper in a chip shop. I made a few enquiries as to where I could get bed and breakfast and was directed to Hyde Road. I went there and stayed at No 36. It would be about half past twelve or a quarter to one.

I told the landlord and landlady that I had come to work for Seddons of Hulme. I booked in and signed the register. I only stayed there one night. I have given the black shoes I was wearing in Littlewoods on the Friday

*to a man for the price of a packet of fags. The raincoat
I was wearing on the Friday I borrowed. I have given it
back to an American known to all the boys by the nick-
name of 'Slim'.*

*The witness then said that it was thirteen miles from New
Mills to Piccadilly and that Grafton House was No 67 Hyde
Road, not No 36. He also said that Sinclair's Hotel was in
Brunswick Street.*

Cross-examined by MR BURKE:

MR BURKE: May I see the original statement?

MR JUSTICE SELLERS: Certainly. (*Produced.*)

MR BURKE: When you went to the Salvation Army Hostel
and saw this man, I put it to you that neither in the way you
suggest nor in any other way did he mention a woman?—It
was not the Salvation Army Hostel, sir, it was the Services
hostel.

The Services hostel, yes?—And he did mention a woman.

Is this what he said to you, 'What the fucking hell do you
want me again for?'—No.

Is that what he said?—No, sir.

He was brought to the Police Station and arrived there at
11.30?—Correct, sir.

Where was he then taken, into what part of the Police
office?—To Room 12 at Police Headquarters.

Is that where Inspector Stainton is to be found or was he
there that night?—He was not there when we went in, but
he was there shortly afterwards.

And you were there?—I was there.

What other officers were present?—Detective Sergeant
Gallimore, Detective Sergeant Blakemore.

Were you present throughout the interrogation of this
man?—I was.

How long did that interrogation last?—About two hours,
sir.

Two hours. You have been giving evidence now for forty
minutes. Am I right in saying that you narrated everything
that took place during that conversation in this Court today
in a period of twenty minutes?—No, sir, the statement was
taken down after the two hours.

Was this man questioned until between five and six o'clock
in the morning continuously?—No, sir.

Did he several times, at least twice, ask if he could go to sleep?—No, sir.

Never?—No, sir.

I put it to you that he did?—No, sir.

And that Inspector Stainton said, 'You will get no sleep till it is cleared up'.—No, sir.

Did he say that?—No, sir, he did not.

Did Inspector Stainton put some photographs in front of him?—He showed him the photographs, as I have related, sir.

In the early stages of the interrogation did he show him, without any hesitation, some photographs?—No, he had some hesitation in showing the photographs at all, and then he showed him one of the deceased's clothing and later showed him the other two of the deceased after death.

Which other two?—The two I have spoken to, in Exhibit No 2.

Did the Inspector put down on the desk, or table, or whatever it was, photographs of this dead woman, and say, 'That is your handiwork, you know'?—No.

The first witness, Police Constable Martin, who gave evidence as to photographs, produced in this Court yesterday two photographs which were not produced at the Police Court?—Yes.

Do you know the ones I am referring to?—Yes.

And one is a picture, is it not, of the whole of this woman's body lying on a mortuary slab, with the head to the left and feet to the right?—As far as I remember, yes.

And the other is a picture of the upper part of the woman's body with the arm thrown back so that some of the under arm hair is visible?—Possibly, sir.

Those were never produced at the Police Court, were they?

MR JUSTICE SELLERS: I think they must be produced now. It is no good describing them. If you want them you must have them. (*Photographs put in and marked Exhibit 37.*)

MR JUSTICE SELLERS: Do you want the jury to have them?

MR BURKE: I do not want unnecessarily to put before the jury things that are gruesome.

MR JUSTICE SELLERS: I think you can leave it at the moment. We have got the photographs identified now.

You know the photographs which are being referred to?—Yes, I do.

MR BURKE: As they were not exhibited at the Police Court the accused could not have seen them there, could he?—No.

Were they put before him by Inspector Stainton, those photographs?—No, sir.

Did the Inspector——? —They were not.

They were not?—No.

Can you think how it is that Rowland is able to instruct his Solicitor with a complete description of those photographs if he has never seen them?—No.

MR JUSTICE SELLERS: What does 'No' mean?—He may very well have seen them, sir.

MR BURKE: Where—in the office?—Room 12, Police Headquarters.

Are photographs of this kind left about so that people can casually glance at them?—Well, they were.

At Police Headquarters?—Well, they were on Detective Stainton's desk.

Were they?—Yes.

Did Inspector Stainton say to this man, 'You know, you have got an uncontrollable temper'?—No, sir.

You say those words came from this man's mouth, do you not?—Yes.

I am suggesting to you they were words used by Inspector Stainton?—They were not, sir.

And that the Inspector said, showing him these gruesome photographs, 'That is your handiwork. You know, you have got an uncontrollable temper'.—No, sir.

You have been quoting from a note of the conversation which took place?—Yes.

When was that note made?—While the conversation was taking place.

As it was proceeding?—Yes.

Is it in shorthand or are they longhand notes?—Longhand.

Were those people conveniently speaking at dictation speed?—Well, more or less. Inspector Stainton was taking notes himself of the conversation.

Your word agrees word for word, does it not, with that of Detective Inspector Stainton's—I could not say.

Did you hear his evidence?—In the Court below, yes.

Why do you say you cannot say whether or not your evidence respecting that conversation agrees word for word with this?—Because I have not checked my note with his evidence.

Because what?—Because I have not checked my note with his evidence.

Have you not compared notes over this case?—No.

When I say compared notes, I do not mean that in the general sense. Have you compared your notes of the conversation one with another?—No, sir.

And is that why they agree word for word?—I have not said they agree word for word. I do not know whether they do or not, but this is the note I took at the time the conversation was taking place.

It would be a singular thing, would it not, if two people taking down a lengthy conversation got the conversation word for word without a syllable of difference. Do not you think that would be an extraordinary thing?—No, sir.

Were Rowland's possessions taken from him?—Yes, sir.

Was this amongst them, a Ministry of Labour card? (*Produced.*) I could not say, sir.

Who took charge of his possessions?—Detective Sergeant Trippier.

We shall hear him in due course. Do you know that Inspector Stainton took possession of a letter from this man's pocket which had been written to his mother?—No, sir, I do not know that.

Did Inspector Stainton tell him that if he made a clean breast of it he would see he only got charged with manslaughter?—No.

I suggest that this man never at any time said that he had a fighting chance?—He said that, sir.

Did Inspector Stainton tell him this: 'I know you have a violent temper and that some people are afraid of you'?—No, sir.

And did this man throughout that interview persistently protest that he was innocent of this crime?—No, sir, he did not.

Did Inspector Stainton say, 'There is a right and a wrong way to plead provocation'?—No, sir.

Then a man came in and asked Rowland, did he not, to show him his finger nails?—No, sir, I was not——.

You never saw that?—No, sir.

Was there any official from the Forensic Laboratory present?—Present where?

On the night of the arrest, the 26th?—No, sir.

You were present during the whole of the interview with Inspector Stainton, were not you?—Yes.

Re-examined by MR NIELD:

Mr Nimmo, although the admissibility of this man's statement has not been questioned, you have been asked a lot of questions about the words used by Detective Inspector Stainton?—Yes.

I want you to tell my Lord and the Jury this. Was there any promise held out to the prisoner?—None whatever, sir.

Was he threatened in any way before he made this statement orally and in writing?—No, sir.

Was there any persuasion used to make him speak?—None whatever, sir.

SERGEANT JOSEPH BLAKEMORE, *detective sergeant attached to 'G' Division, Manchester Police, examined by* MR NIELD, *said that he went with Detective Constable Nimmo on 26 October at about 11 pm to see Rowland at the Services' Transit Dormitory. He said that Nimmo woke up Rowland and asked him to get dressed and that Rowland then said, 'You don't want me for murdering that fucking woman, do you?' He said that he was then cautioned and that he later said, 'Is it about that coat?' He said that he was then taken to Police Headquarters.*

In cross-examination by MR BURKE *it was put to him that Rowland never mentioned the woman. He said that he did. It was suggested that the question that Rowland asked was, 'What the fucking hell do you want me for?' when he was speaking to Detective Constable Nimmo whom he knew. The witness denied that that was what he said.*

SERGEANT EMRYS JONES TRIPPIER, *detective sergeant in the Manchester Police, examined by* MR NIELD, *said that he was the police officer who dealt with all the exhibits.*

DR JAMES BRIERLEY FIRTH, *Director of the Home Office Laboratory at Preston, examined by* MR NIELD, *said that on*

*Rowland's left shoe on the vertical edge of the inside of the
left heel there was a blood stain which he was able to identify
as human blood but there was insufficient of it to group it.
He said that at its highest point it would be about five-
eighths of an inch above the level of the ground. He further
said that in the turn-up of Rowland's trousers there was a
quantity of debris containing fragments of brick dust,
cement, charcoal, clinker and withered leaf tissue. He also
gave evidence that a sample taken from the site of the murder
was similar to that which was found in Rowland's turn-up.*

Cross-examined by MR BURKE *he agreed that it was reasonable to expect that sort of debris in any blitzed site. He said
that he made a very careful examination of Rowland's clothes
and that he was not able to detect on the clothes a single
speck of blood.*

The cross-examination continued as follows:

MR BURKE: The woman's garments were heavily blood-
stained, were they not?—Yes, in positions consistent with the
injuries.

And you have seen those dreadful photographs, have you,
doctor?—I have seen the photographs, yes.

She must have lost a lot of blood?—In time.

In time?—Yes.

She would stop bleeding when she was dead, would not
she?—Yes.

Because the heart stops pumping the blood, doesn't it,
when a person dies?—Yes.

And the process of killing this woman, whoever did it,
would not have taken very long, would it, having regard to
all the circumstances?—No.

So that all the blood which escaped from her body must
have escaped in a very short space of time, do not you agree?
—I do not, no. I do not know how long she lived after she
received her injuries.

Is not it obvious that she must have died from one or
another of those blows at the time when the blow was
inflicted?—No, not obvious at all.

You heard Dr Jenkins's evidence, the bone smashed round
one eye, the brain protruding, the skull fractured. Is not it
quite clear that the woman must have died while those blows
were being rained upon her?—No, not at all; it does not

follow in the least—may have lived for quite an appreciable time.

If I may say so, with respect, you are not a Doctor of Medicine?—No, but I have seen murders committed with hammers where the person ultimately bled to death, even with the brain protruding.

There was blood on a concrete block, was not there?—Yes.

Which was found near this woman's body?—Yes, I found it.

And that blood escaped at some time or another, but there is none upon this man's clothes?—That is so, but that does not mean anything.

Does not mean anything?—Not necessarily.

Why do you say that?—Because a person can produce those injuries on another person it is not necessary for that person to have on his or her clothing blood spots.

But if he had had blood on his clothing that would have been important, something to think about, would it not?— But the absence of it is not elimination.

Did you hear the evidence of Dr Jenkins?—Yes.

A distinguished pathologist?—Yes.

Did you hear him say that he had had considerable experience?—Yes.

As a medical man?—Yes.

Of cases involving violence?—Yes.

Did you hear him say that it was improbable that a man could have committed a deed such as this and not have had blood on his clothes?—He said it was improbable. I do not use the word 'impossible'. I say 'improbable'.

Do you think an improbability of that kind in a case of this kind means nothing?—Is that what you are seriously telling the members of the jury?—There are quite a number of factors which must be taken into consideration in an assault of this type. When a weapon of this type is used, if it strikes certain muscular parts of the body there is no pronounced escape of blood at the time of the blow. In order to get an escape of blood at the time of the blow it is necessary to rupture comparatively major blood-vessels, and the direction in which that blood will be ejected from the surface depends upon a number of factors: it depends upon the direction of the blow, the actual contact—a hammer head in this case—with the surface. It depends upon the distance at

G

which that blow was given and it also depends upon the relative position of the assailant and the aggrieved person. I am not at all surprised that a person could—I say that a person could—inflict those injuries on another and yet bear no trace of the injuries on himself.

So it is all guesswork?—It is not guesswork at all. If a person strikes someone else with an instrument of this sort on a muscular part of the body, unless they have penetrated severely, they are not blood-letting injuries. What happens when you first strike a muscular part of the body—the muscle is filled with tiny capillaries, not blood vessels—is that the capillaries are compressed, and that results in other vessels, blood vessels, rupturing—and that is what happens when the eye goes black, when someone gets a black eye.

Are you suggesting that the injuries inflicted in this case are not blood-letting injuries?—Not in the real sense of the word. With the exception of the blows here (*indicating*) the blows that killed this woman are not what I should call rapidly blood-letting injuries.

They are blood-letting injuries. The photographs point to the fact that blood has been let.—In due course.

Did you hear Dr Jenkins in his evidence say that the blow which smashed the bone near the eye had ruptured a number of veins?—I agree, yes.

And would cause spurting blood. Did you hear him say that?—In my opinion it does not follow that the assailant ever felt spurting blood.

He must have been near the woman, whoever he was, must he not, in order to strike her with the hammer at all?—Yes, but the spurts are directional. I have had experience of cases where a hammer has been used where the amount of spurting blood has been comparatively negligible, and the assailant has had none on him.

When was the last time that you had a case of that kind?—The case I am thinking of in particular is a case where a man was murdered in Blackpool.

A man murdered in Blackpool?—Yes, where he received 7 or 8 head injuries as the result of a hammer blow.

Inflicted with what?—A hammer. The assailant was a woman and there was no blood on her clothing.

A woman hit him?—Yes, and the head injuries were severe.

But you would not expect a woman to be able to hit a person with the same degree of force as a man?—Well, he had a fractured skull and the brain was protruding.

What about the veins? Were the veins ruptured in such a way as to cause the spurting of blood?—Tiny splashes on the wall.

Many?—Some half-dozen.

I am putting it to you that if you would regard the presence of blood on this man's clothes as of importance, then surely the absence of blood is equally as important?—I agree it is of some importance, but what I say is that the absence of blood is not necessarily elimination.

You say it is of some importance now. Did not you say earlier that it means nothing?—I may casually have used that word to stress that it did not provide elimination.

However, we have got this far, that it is of some importance?—There is no blood on his clothing.

Re-examined by MR NIELD:

You have been asked about guesswork, and so on. How long have you been doing this sort of investigation for the Home Office?—Approximately nine years, nine or ten years.

And you are directing from their premises at the laboratory at Preston?—That is so.

Have you had many or a few cases in which you have been asked to investigate scientifically?—A very considerable number.

DETECTIVE INSPECTOR FRANK STAINTON, *detective inspector, Manchester Police, examined by* MR NIELD, *said that he was the officer in charge of the case. He went to the scene of the murder on Sunday, 20 October, at 11.45 am. He gave evidence of Rowland's interview on 26 October at 11.30 pm at the police station. His evidence on this matter was similar to that of Detective Constable Nimmo. He also said that Rowland was the only man who had been detained on suspicion of causing Olive Balchin's death.*

[He was cross-examined on behalf of Rowland at considerable length but, as no submission was made that what Rowland said to him was not admissible in evidence and as a good deal of the cross-examination was about the book at the boarding house at 81 Brunswick Street which is difficult to understand without the book being produced and as none of

the witness's answers, except for the statements which he said Rowland had made and which have already been given in Detective Constable Nimmo's evidence, suggested either Rowland's guilt or his innocence, the cross-examination has been omitted.]

MR NIELD: My Lord, that is the case for the Crown.

MR BURKE *opened the case for the Defence.*

EVIDENCE FOR THE DEFENCE

WALTER GRAHAM ROWLAND, *the accused, then gave evidence.*

Examined by MR BURKE:

MR BURKE: Did you batter this woman to death with a hammer, as is alleged in this case?

ROWLAND: I swear before Almighty God that I did not.

ROWLAND *then said that in November 1945 he was released from the Forces and staying at home with his parents. He said he had never used grease as a dressing for his hair but that while he was on leave his mother gave him a bottle of brilliantine. He confirmed her evidence that he had said he didn't use such stuff and had given it to his brother. He said that he knew Olive Balchin and that on the day of his arrest he knew that he had venereal disease for which he had had treatment for the first time that night, that was Saturday, 26 October. He affirmed that the disease was in its secondary stage, that he had had intercourse with women in Italy when he was in the Forces and that it was in fact impossible for him to have got the disease from Olive Balchin. He agreed that he did not know that on 19 October and that he suspected her of having given it to him.*

He said that on 19 October he visited his parents' house, as his mother had said, and that he went to New Mills from the bus station at Lower Moseley Street. He said that he caught the 6.15 bus from that bus station. He said that he went to the bus station from the GPO, Spring Gardens, where he had called to see if there was a parcel of washing sent to him by his mother, but it was not there. He said that he called at the GPO at about twenty past five. He said that he was then wearing a blue pinstripe suit and brown shoes, the suit which was produced by the police and which was taken off him while he was in custody. He said that he had no other suit at that time and that it was his demob suit and that the suit that he was wearing at the trial was one lent to him by the police.

He said that the collar he was wearing when he went to his parents was pale brown with a stripe in it and there was a shirt to match. He said he had no grease on his hair that night and that he was not wearing a mackintosh. He said that at his parents' house he changed his shirt, collar, socks, vest and underpants and that the shirt which he put on was a light blue shirt. He said he took his coat off in order to wash while he was there and put it over a chair. He said there was no hammer in the pocket of the jacket or in any other pocket of any garment which he was wearing, either while he was at his mother's house or at any time that day. He said he had never seen the hammer which the police produced before it was produced to him at the office in the police station.

MR BURKE: Is Mr MacDonald right when he says that you had bought it at his shop?

ROWLAND: Definitely not. I had never seen Mr MacDonald in my life until I saw him at that identification parade.

He said that he left his mother's house at a quarter past nine and caught a bus at half past nine. He thought that it was going through to Manchester and did not know that it went to Stockport until he had been on it for some time. He got off at Stockport at Mersey Square. After getting off, first of all he went round to the back of the bus station into the gents' toilet and from there round the corner again and into the bottom Wellington hotel. He said that there was a bar in the bottom Wellington and that he went into it. He said he had three glasses of beer and that he went to the gents' toilet in the public house. He said that he definitely remembered seeing two police officers walking out of the door as he was coming back from the gents' toilet. They were in uniform and he distinctly saw their helmets. He said that was just about half past ten, because just before he went out the bar stopped selling any more beer.

He said he left the premises not more than five minutes after he had seen the police officers, walked across to Mersey Square to the bus stop on the opposite side from the Touch-stone hotel and waited there for a bus. He waited about ten minutes and caught a bus going to Manchester. When he left his mother's house and in the Wellington hotel he was carrying a parcel which contained his overalls and shirt. It was definitely not a thin, long parcel such as might have contained a hammer or something of that kind. He caught the bus and got off it on the Manchester side of Ardwick Green. He believed the road going from it was called Rusholme Road but he wasn't sure. This was shortly after 11 pm and not more than five past eleven. He said that the bus stop was at the other end of Ardwick Green from Brunswick Street. He walked back along Ardwick towards Ardwick Green and turned round by the garage to Brunswick Street. He had intended getting off the bus before he got there but it was a limited stop bus and he missed the other corner and had to go on to the corner of Rusholme Road.

In Brunswick Street he went into a chip shop and bought some chips, then he went on to the opposite side of the road and asked a soldier if he could tell him where he could find a place to get bed and breakfast. The soldier directed him to a row of houses where he said quite a few people took in casual people for the night. He said that he went there and rang the bell at one house and a gentleman came to the door and he asked him if he could accommodate him for the night and he said he could. This was in Brunswick Street. He had stayed in that house before. When he saw the man in the light he recognised him. He didn't know the number of the house and he did not remember it when he was giving evidence. He said that he caught a glimpse of a small enamelled plate screwed to the door, white enamel, and on that it said NO CANVASSERS.

He did not know the name of the man who answered the door until he was in court that day. He said he signed his name in the visitors' book. The book was produced to the witness and he identified his signature. He said that the man he now knew to be Beaumont put the date in. He said that Beaumont also filled in the date on which he left. He said that he stayed there one night only. A room was allotted to him, namely the middle room on the ground floor. He arrived at the house at about 11.15 pm. Having arrived there he decided to go out for a short time to get a drink or something to take the taste of the fat of the chips out of his mouth.

He wanted some mineral water. He thought he might get some at the chip shop. Before he went out he told Beaumont that he was going to try and get a drink and asked if it was all right. Beaumont said 'Yes, but I may be in bed so you'd better take the key'. He gave the witness the key. He said he went to the chip shop but it was closed and he returned to the house. He was definitely not away from the house for more than ten minutes. The landlord was still up and said that he was back quickly and he gave him back the key as soon as he came in. He said that he had never had that key in his possession from that time onward.

The next morning Beaumont brought water to him and a lady brought his breakfast. He said that he was in bed when Beaumont brought the water but that when the lady came he was not. He had his singlet and trousers on. His shirt was over the chair and it was the pale blue shirt which he put on when he came away from his mother's. He said that he showed Beaumont the card which he had had from the labour exchange. The card directed him to a place to get employment, namely a firm called Seddons. It was dated 11 October and was from the Ministry of Labour and National Service. It ran as follows:

> In reply to your request for a joiner. I am sending you the bearer Mr W. G. Rowland. Please complete this part and return by return of post. No stamp is required.

At the bottom was the address of the firm, Messrs Seddon, Great Jackson Street, Hulme, Manchester. Rowland said he was sure that that was the card he showed to Beaumont and that he still had the parcel which he had got from his mother's when he arrived at Beaumont's house. He said that he left Beaumont's house at about 10 am on the 20th October. That was a Sunday. He said that the first person he told about his being in that house was his solicitor, Mr Hinchcliffe. He said that he definitely was not in MacDonald's shop and did not buy the hammer. He said that he had never seen Olive Balchin on that day or night and that he was never in the Queen's café that night.

MR BURKE: We have heard the evidence of a witness who says you were there between 10.30 and 11 o'clock.—I definitely was not there.

And she says you were there in the presence of two women?
—I was never there, either alone or with anyone else.

He said that he had not been at the Queen's café on Satur-
day, 19 October, either in the day or at night, but that he
had been there before.

MR BURKE: And another witness says that going along
Deansgate towards midnight he saw a man and a woman
quarrelling at the corner of Cumberland Street and he
identified you as the man?—He is mistaken, sir, I was asleep
in bed then.

Were you ever at the corner of Cumberland Street that
night?—I was never in the centre of Manchester or that
locality after a quarter past six.

He said that at 11 pm on 26 October he was woken up by
Detective Constable Nimmo and Sergeant Blakemore.

MR BURKE: He says that, using an obscene expression, you
said, 'You don't want me for murdering that woman, do
you?' Did you ever speak about a woman to the officer?—I
am quite aware the police officers have made that statement
and in the face of that I say now, in front of this court, I did
not say that.

Did you say anything about a woman at all?—I did not.

What did you say?—I did come out with the obscene
remark but not in the sentence they say I came out with.
When I woke up I knew him and he knew me, but I was
annoyed to think I was being pestered with him and I asked
him, using the remark, what he wanted me again for.

And he says that you said something like this: 'Is it
about that coat?'—I did say that.

He said that he was then taken to the police station and
interrogated.

THIRD DAY *Saturday, 14 December 1946*

Continuing his evidence in chief, ROWLAND *said that the*
interrogation went on until about four in the morning, that
at least twice he asked if he could have some sleep and that
INSPECTOR STAINTON *said that there would be no sleep until*
the matter was cleared up. That he was shown two photo-
graphs of a woman's head and both of them had injuries on

them and he said that INSPECTOR STAINTON *said to him, 'That
is your handiwork'. He said that he told* INSPECTOR STAINTON
that he had no knowledge whatever about the affair.

MR BURKE: The inspector has told the Court that he asked
you to give an account of your movements on Saturday, the
19th, and Sunday, the 20th October. He says you replied,
'I'm admitting nothing. It is only a fool's game to do that.'
Did you say that?—Those words were spoken by me but not
in the circumstances in which they appear in the evidence
... they were used by me under the circumstances I am going
to relate now. Detective Inspector Stainton had been questioning me for some time and all his questions were not in
regard to this woman's death. He had been questioning me
in regard to why I had been living in Manchester under the
conditions that I was—no settled address. I tried to explain
that was purely a private and domestic matter. The sugges-
tion was made that I had been living on my wits, my lord.
That was when I said I am admitting nothing. That is only
a fool's game.

Was it said in answer to a question such as this? 'Do you
care to give me an account of your movements on Saturday,
the 19th, and Sunday, the 20th October?'—Definitely not, sir.

Was it said in answer to any questions specifically relating
to this woman's death?—Not at all, sir.

The inspector has told the court you went on to say 'I can
account for where I was'. Did you say that at any stage of the
conversation?—I did.

Was that said at the same time or a different time from
the time when you said 'I am admitting nothing. It's only a
fool's game to do that'?—It was a different time altogether.

Were the words, 'I can account for where I was' in answer
to any question?—No direct question, no.

'I can account for where I was.' What were you referring
to, what time or day?—Well, the whole topic of conversation
was in regard to the night of 19 October.

And did those words relate to that night or not?—Definitely they related to that night.

The inspector has told the court that you then said, 'I was
at home at New Mills when she was murdered'. Did you say
that?—I don't recollect saying that—he had not stated any
definite time when she was murdered. He had told me

it was between 11 o'clock that night and 11 o'clock on the 20th.

He says you told him, 'I was at home in New Mills when she was murdered'. You say you can't remember saying that? —I do not remember saying those words.

And he says you went on to say, 'I did not come back to Manchester that night'. Did you say that?—It's very probable I did say that but not as it is down there after I had made the other remark.

When you say it is probable that you said that, can you remember definitely whether you said it or whether you didn't say it?—I remember definitely I said it in the statement.

In your written statement?—Yes.

Whether it was said in your statement or at any other time, if it is said what did it mean? 'I didn't come back to Manchester that night'?—My reference to Manchester I was implying my term there as Manchester meant the centre of the town. I was no nearer Manchester that night than Ardwick Green.

At the time when you said that, had you or had you not been told about the place in which this woman's body had been found?—Oh yes, sir.

The inspector has told the members of the jury that he then said to you, 'Do you care to tell me where you stayed on the Saturday night, the 19th October?' Did he ask you that question?—He had asked me that, yes.

And that in answer to that question you said, 'Have you seen my mother?' Did you at any stage of the conversation say, 'Have you seen my mother?'—I did.

Was that said as the inspector stated in answer to the question, 'Do you care to tell me where you stayed on the Saturday night, the 19th October?'—Do you mean in answer to that question?

Were the words, 'Have you seen my mother?' said in answer to that question or were they not?—Definitely not, sir.

Were they said in relation to any question which was addressed to you by the police?—No, sir, it was just a request. It was me that asked them if they had seen my mother.

Inspector Stainton said that whenever the question was

asked, 'Have you seen my mother?', that he replied, 'No, not yet'. Did he reply to those words?—No, he did not.

The inspector's evidence is to this effect, that you said to him, 'Well, I did come back to Manchester. I got a lift in a car and went to a pub for a drink'. Did you say that?—I have no recollection of ever mentioning a car . . .

Did you say, 'Well, I did come back to Manchester'?—I have no recollection of saying that, sir.

Did you say, 'I got a lift in a car'?—Definitely not.

Did you say to the inspector that you got a lift in a car and went to a pub for a drink?—No, sir, not to the best of my knowledge I did not say anything about being in a pub.

Did you say, 'I did not go into Deansgate'?—Yes. I emphaticaly stated that, sir.

Had Deansgate been mentioned?—Oh, definitely, sir.

By whom?—By Detective Inspector Stainton.

Did you say, 'I stayed in the Ardwick district'?—Yes, sir.

Was that true?—Quite true, sir . . .

Was it or was it not true that you stayed at the Grafton House in Hyde Road on the night in question?—Well, I believed it to be true when I said it.

Do you now know whether it was accurate or inaccurate? —I now know that I had made an honest mistake.

Did you say, 'I didn't get in till after one o'clock'?—Yes, very possibly I did.

At any time near the time when this woman met her death had you stayed at the Grafton House in Hyde Road?—Yes, I now know that I stayed there on the Sunday.

And on the Sunday when you stayed at the Grafton House in Hyde Road at what time did you get in at night to that place?—Well, I'm not sure.

Was it early or late?—It would be latish. Getting late at night.

The inspector then said he told you it would be necessary to make enquiries at that address to prove your statement. Did he say that?—He didn't say that to me. I heard him instruct two detectives to go to the house.

. . . did the inspector make it clear as to what his intention was respecting that address in Hyde Road?—Oh yes, sir.

To have enquiries made?—Oh yes, I follow what you mean, sir.

Inspector Stainton has said that when that situation arose you said, 'Well, I didn't stay there'. Is that correct?—I was never asked any more whether I stayed there until those detectives came back . . .

Did you say to Inspector Stainton, referring to Grafton House, 'Well, I didn't stay there'?—No, sir. I was of the firm opinion at the time that I had stayed there.

And did you go on to say, 'I stayed at 36 Hyde Road and only stayed there for one night'?—I did refer to Hyde Road.

Did you refer to 36 Hyde Road?—I do not recollect any number.

Did you tell the inspector at any stage of the conversation that you had stayed on the night in question in Hyde Road? —Yes, I may have suggested it after the detectives came back and said that I had not been at the other place . . . Grafton House . . .

What happened when they came back? Did the inspector say anything in your presence?—They had a whispered conversation.

Following upon the whispered conversation was something said to you?—It was, sir.

What was said?—Detective Inspector Stainton turned to me after this conversation and said, 'Just as I thought. You never did stay there that night'.

What did you say in answer to that statement?—I replied I was still convinced I had stayed there that night.

Where?—At Grafton House.

Did you or did you not believe that to be true?—I did. At the time you said it?—I did.

ROWLAND *then said that he told Inspector Stainton that he had known Olive Balchin for about eight weeks and he had known her as 'Lil'. He said to the inspector, 'I made sure that she did not know my name'. He said to the inspector, 'Things like that do not happen to decent women' and that whoever did it didn't do it without a cause.*

MR BURKE: Did you say, 'You cannot see what you've done in the dark'?—Inspector Stainton said to me, 'It must prick his conscience'. He was referring to the photograph.

Yes?—In the conversation after that I passed the remark that no one could have seen what they had done in the dark . . .

\

The inspector says that he showed you two photographs taken after the woman was dead. Is that true?—I did see two photographs.

And you said, so the inspector alleges, 'Yes, that is her, but I've got a fighting chance and I'm going to hang on to it'.— No recollection of using those terms. Nothing about the fighting chance.

Did you say, 'I've got an uncontrollable temper but that isn't evidence, is it?'—I did not say that, sir.

Were the words 'uncontrollable temper' used by anyone? —Yes, Inspector Stainton passed the remark and I replied 'that is not evidence'.

MR JUSTICE SELLERS: Passed what remark?

ROWLAND: He said he knew I had an uncontrollable temper, my Lord.

MR BURKE: And you replied—'That is not evidence'?

ROWLAND: I did.

MR BURKE: Did you say, 'I am sure I wouldn't do that'?— I did. As I said it I was pointing to the photographs.

Did you say it is possible the hammer was got to do a job with?—Yes, sir.

Did you say 'I was not going to do a job that night'?—I did, sir.

Did you add this. 'The fact that I went home proves that'? —I did, sir.

I just want you to listen to the whole of the sentence. Did you say this or part of it? 'The fact that I went home proves that, unless you think I could do the job when I came back'? —No, sir.

Did you say any part of that?—I said part of that, yes, sir.

What part did you say?—The fact that when I spoke about going to New Mills, the fact that I had been to New Mills proved that.

Did you say, 'I am not admitting anything'?—Not to my recollection, sir. I had nothing to admit. My conscience was perfectly clear.

Did you say, 'I came back on the 9.30 bus from New Mills and got off at Ardwick'?—I made that statement. That was the latter end of the interrogation.

ROWLAND *said that he had never been near Deansgate on that Saturday. He said the inspector asked him if he was wearing a raincoat and he said that he was wearing this suit. He told him that he had had a mac which he had borrowed from a man whom he knew as 'Slim' but it was not in reference to having it on that day. It was in reference to an occasion earlier in the week when he was in company of this fellow and wanted to go round to the GPO. He said he was in the NAAFI with him and it was raining and he wanted to go to the GPO and that Slim lent him his raincoat and that he gave it him back within the hour.*

ROWLAND *agreed that he said it was a blow to find that he had VD and that he had a pride in his body and that he would have liked to know where he had got it. He agreed that he said, 'If I had been sure it was her I would have strangled her', and that for all he knew it may have been her. He also said to the inspector that if she had given him VD she deserved all she got.*

ROWLAND *then dealt with the identification parade and with the alleged failure by MacDonald to identify him in the Police Court. [As Mr Hinchcliffe was present on that occasion and failed to give evidence to support Rowland's version of what happened, my own view is that MacDonald's version should be accepted, but what follows is what Rowland said about it.]*

MR BURKE: Would you tell my Lord and the jury whether or not MacDonald picked you out in Court as the man who bought the hammer?—He did not pick me out until I was pointed out to him.

MacDonald has said in his evidence before the members of the jury that he was asked by Prosecuting Counsel whether he could see the man in Court who had bought the hammer. You agree with MacDonald that that question was addressed to him?—Yes, sir.

And he has also said that in answer to that question he said No?—He said he could not see the man.

He said he could not see the man. And he has told my Lord and the jury that the reason he could not see the man was because you were keeping your head down?—I heard him give that evidence, yes.

Is that true?—Definitely not true.

How did you look at him—did you look at him when he——?—When I saw the hesitation he made I was looking at him then, and when I saw the hesitation he made I turned round to Mr Hinchcliffe to try and draw his attention to the fact he could not pick me out and Mr Hinchcliffe was looking at me, and I looked back again at MacDonald.

So far as you could see, did MacDonald look at you?—He definitely looked all round the Court.

Yes, I know that, but did he look at you?—Certainly.

Did you do anything at all to prevent him having a complete view of your face?—Certainly not, sir.

When Mr MacDonald had looked round the Court, and had told the learned Stipendiary—the Magistrate—that he could not see the man in Court, do you remember the question which was then addressed——?—I remember it perfectly.

To Mr MacDonald, by Prosecuting Counsel?—I remember perfectly what happened.

Now, tell my Lord and the jury, quite slowly, what happened?—My Lord, when MacDonald made his remark to the Magistrate that he could not see the man, the gentleman who was conducting the Prosecution—and I remember this quite clearly my Lord—said: 'I will approach it from another angle'. He asked him if he had identified the man who had bought the hammer, at an identification parade. MacDonald replied that he had, and the gentleman for the Prosecution then turned round and pointed to me and said: 'Is that the man?' MacDonald then asked me to stand up.

Who did?—MacDonald did.

Yes?—Then he said—'Yes'.

And during that questioning to which you have just referred, did anyone point in your direction?—Definitely.

Who?—The gentleman who was taking the Prosecution.

How far away from you was he when he pointed to you? —Well, if I was sat in the position of Mr Hinchcliffe now, the gentleman that turned round and pointed to me would be about half past to your right as you stand there now.

Like *that*?—Yes, sir.

MR JUSTICE SELLERS: That is in the front row, just to your right?—He was in the row in front of me, that is quite correct, my Lord.

In cross-examination by MR NIELD, *Rowland was asked*:
Do you at this moment take the view that if you had con-

tracted venereal disease from this woman she deserved all she got?—I don't take that view now.

What has happened to change your view?—The circumstances that have elapsed since.

What circumstances?—I am stood in this court on a charge of murder. Is not that sufficient circumstances when a man has a clear conscience and has to stand there and hear evidence in court and his life juggled with?

Do you mean by that that now, faced with the murder charge you see now it may be damaging to you to say that she deserved all she got?—I have admitted that I said that.

But you said more than that, didn't you? To the police you said, 'If I had been sure it was her, I would have strangled her'.—Certainly I said that, yes, it is quite true.

Did you mean that too?—When I said it I meant it, sir . . .

Look at the third paragraph of your statement. Did you say, 'It was in my mind to try and find out whether she had this complaint'?—That is quite right.

'Without letting her know'?—That is quite right.

Who is she?—Olive Balchin.

. . . That meant of course that you suspected that it might be she?—Yes, I will grant you that.

Do not grant me anything. Just tell the truth, if you will. Is that right?—Yes, but I had no more reason to suspect her than any other woman.

But along with others or perhaps with one other in Trafford Park, you wanted to find out if she had got it?—Yes, quite true.

He agreed that late at night it would be dark on the bombed site where the woman was murdered and that anybody on that plot of land couldn't very well see what he was doing . . .

MR NIELD: Did you mean no one in the dark can see the extent of the injuries they inflict?—Maybe that was what I had in mind.

Why did you say that?—As I have just explained, in the face of the remark which was passed about the sight of this woman's injuries pricking the conscience. They don't prick my conscience because I didn't cause them . . .

You know, I suggest, that the principal object of the police was to find out from you where you spent the night. Do you think so?—Yes, I came to that conclusion naturally because I was asked.

But I want you to tell my lord and the jury this. During the police investigation during the preliminary enquiry before the magistrate and right up to the time you see your solicitor, have you ever before said that you were at 81 Brunswick Street?—When I was taken in front of the magistrate on the Monday morning, the 28th October, the stipendiary magistrate appointed Mr Hinchcliffe to look after my interests and I had a conversation with Mr Hinchcliffe that day and he paid a visit to me in the prison and I told Mr Hinchcliffe that I had stayed in a place in the Ardwick district and that I couldn't say the address or what it was. What would the police have said if I had explained a 'bull' story like this?

What sort of story?—If I had turned round and said 'I don't know the address or the people', what would they have thought about it?

Isn't that better than lying about it?—It was not lying. What I said was said in all sincerity. What I said at the time I had no reason to believe it was different.

You mean that?—I mean that.

You knew that a woman had died, clearly murdered. You are being asked to account for your movements on a special night. Do you say that you cannot after all the hours that have passed according to you at the police station cast your mind back five nights, six nights, seven nights?—I heard the police give evidence that the interrogation only lasted two hours.

Could you not in those circumstances cast your mind back seven nights?—Not at first, I couldn't.

Why did you then tell them an address which is quite incorrect?—Because I thought at the time I definitely stayed there on that Saturday night. It was my honest belief when I said to the police that I had stayed at that address that I had stayed at that address on Saturday night. It was an honest mistake.

It's two mistakes, isn't it?—It appears that I made quite a few mistakes.

But on this particular occasion did you tell the police you stayed at Grafton House?—Yes.

That is wrong, isn't it?—Yes, I know it to be wrong now, but when I said it it was my firm belief that it was true.

Did you then tell them that you had stayed at 36 Hyde Road?—I never actually recollect mentioning the number, but I do recollect mentioning Hyde Road because I have stayed in Hyde Road . . .

Brunswick Street is, according to you, the true place where you did stay?—Yes.

You told us a moment ago that it would be a 'bull' story—I think that was the phrase—to tell the police. Did you not know the number or the address or anything of that kind? Didn't you?—Yes, sir.

Do you mean by that that you purposely refrained from telling the police, 'Well, this was up Brunswick Street, I don't know the number'. Because you thought you wouldn't be believed?—Not at first. But I did after. I adopted that attitude after.

After when?—After a man had walked into a police court yard and identified me, whom I knew in my own conscience that I had never seen before in my life. It was after that that I thought it better in my own interest to keep the knowledge of where I had been to myself until I had seen a legal adviser.

. . . During your interrogation by Inspector Stainton you decided to keep the information to yourself as to where you had stayed because you could not give the address?—I did.

And it follows from that perfectly clearly, does it not, that you knew Grafton House and 36 Hyde Road were untrue?—Not until after the interrogation had finished and the identification parade.

You were preserving to yourself the true place because you thought that the police would not believe you?—That was definitely my reason . . .

. . . Would you look at the book? And at an entry in August. I think it's the 14th . . . What is the name of the visitor in that place?—My own name.

Wait a minute?—14 August. My name is there in my handwriting. Walter Graham Rowland.

Did you stay there on 14 August?—I did.

Then why did you say you couldn't identify the place sufficiently to satisfy the police?—I still say I couldn't identify the place because I had been to a place once, late at night in a street like Brunswick Street.

Two months before?—Yes, two months before. I couldn't think where I was that night a week after, not two months after . . . It would have been far better for me to have been able to tell the police immediately instead of being charged and held in custody and going through this ordeal. I know in my own conscience and I am the only one in this court who does know that I am totally innocent of this charge.

On 19/20 October, if you did stay at Brunswick Street, you would remember staying two months before, wouldn't you, in August?—I didn't remember staying at this same address until the man opened the door and we saw each other and he mentioned the fact . . .

You are telling us that on the 26th—when obviously this charge of murder was pending—you couldn't remember or were unwilling to disclose—the place to the police because you thought they wouldn't believe it?—I've already said that at first I made an honest mistake but after I deliberately withheld the information from the police for reasons in regard to my own defence.

Does that book indicate that you left the address on 19 October?—Yes, it does.

Is that true?—No, I left the house on Sunday morning about 10 o'clock.

The 20th?—The 20th. And I did not put that date in the book.

Whoever did is wrong?—Definitely it is not right . . .

After you left the Army and up to 20 October . . . had you one suit or more?—When I came out of the Army—you are speaking now of 18 June—

Yes.—I had two suits.

Did you get rid of one?—I lost one.

When?—Early in July.

From early in July until 26 October was Exhibit 12/13/14 your only suit?—Yes, it was, sir . . .

Two witnesses, whose statements you have asked for by

your counsel and produced have described you as neat and
tidy. Were you neat and tidy?—I always endeavour to be . . .

Can you remember the dates when you had intercourse
with Olive Balchin at Baxendale's site? . . .—I should say
not later than the middle of September.

And in the doorway?—Yes, that was in the early part of
the month as far as I can remember.

The early part of September?—Yes, or the latter part of
August . . .

. . . Look at Exhibit No 34 [Rowland's statement] . . .
is the statement true?—Yes, as far as my power to recall
what is in here, I say it is true . . .

And did you go on to say, 'It was in my mind to try to
find out if she had this complaint without letting her know.
I left there at about a quarter past nine with Lil and left
her at the bottom of the stairs and went down towards
London Road station for a drink at the Feathers. Later
I went to the NAAFI and stayed there. Before I left her
I said I would see her the following night.'?—Yes, sir, but
you asked if I had made arrangements to see her the following night and I had not and did not. It was just a figure of
speech—you say, all right I will see you tomorrow. You
asked if I had made arrangements to see the woman. My
answer is No.

Did you say before leaving her on 18 October you would
see her on 19 October?—Certainly I did. It is in this statement But I didn't arrange to meet her.

Did you intend to meet her?—The thought never entered
my mind. It was a figure of speech. I said, 'I will see you
tomorrow'.

It is not tomorrow, it is tomorrow night?—All right.
Tomorrow night. It is just a figure of speech. I definitely did
not say I will see you at eight o'clock at night or seven
o'clock at night.

Do you mean you had no intention of meeting her?—I
had no intention of meeting her. What more or less would
be in my mind would be I would very likely see her if I
had gone into Littlewoods café.

On 19 October I gather you to say that you at no time
visited the shop of Mr MacDonald.

I have never visited Mr MacDonald's shop in my life . . .

During that day [19th October] you had found out, hadn't you, that you had no money.—Yes, naturally as everyone does. They spend up sometime.

I am not concerned with that—I only want to know the fact for the information of the jury. Had you finished your money?—Yes, that afternoon.

And where did you get some more money, if any?—Off some of my friends.

How much money?—Near enough thirty shillings . . .

You say you got the 6.15 bus and arrived at your parents' house at about half-past seven?—That is it.

When you left at twenty minutes past nine, did you say you were going back to Manchester?—I did.

And that you intended to get the 9.30 bus?—Yes, I did.

Was that true?—Perfectly true.

You intended to go to Manchester?—I intended to get the Manchester bus and come back into Manchester.

But you say you stayed at Stockport, do you?—I got off the bus because it doesn't come through. If the bus had come through to Manchester, I would have stayed in the bus. I had to get out of the bus because it did not go further than Stockport I decided to go to the bottom Wellington for a drink.

You say that if the bus had come on you would have stayed on. Would you have met Lil?—Definitely not.

In spite of the night before, having said you would see her that night?—Definitely not. As I said before, when I said that it was merely a figure of speech and didn't mean a thing.

If it was a figure of speech, why did you put it in your statement?—Because I was writing that statement I was putting in the truth. The fact that I put it in there showed that I had nothing to hide . . .

You have given, have you not, a number of accounts of your movements on the night of 19/20 October?—I have given a number of accounts?

Yes.—I don't quite follow you, sir.

Have you not said first of all that you were at home at New Mills with your parents?—That's quite true.

You knew at the earliest stages of the investigation, did you not, that the times in question were 11 pm on the 19th and 11 am on the 20th?—That is what I was told in the police office, yes.

When you were asked where you had spent the night in question you first of all said, did you not, at home at New Mills?—I said that I had been home that night but I did not say I had stayed there all night.

But didn't you?—I didn't stay there all night, no.

But didn't you say that?—I said that I had been to my parents' home, yes.

Mr Stainton has said that what you said to him was, 'I was at home at New Mills when she was murdered'.—That is what Mr Stainton says I said.

Is it right?—No.

Is it wrong?—How could I say when she was murdered? How could I tell them? He didn't say himself when she was murdered. He only said between eleven at night and eleven the following morning.

Did you go on to say, 'I didn't come back to Manchester that night'?—Yes.

That was not true, was it?—It was true as I meant it. I meant that I was not in Manchester itself. I didn't come any further than Ardwick. When I said Manchester in that sense I meant the centre of the town as I know it. Piccadilly, Market Street and so on . . .

When you told your mother that you were going back to Manchester, you meant to Ardwick, did you?

In the general sense, no. I was going into Manchester when I left my mother. I had full intentions of going into Manchester. If I had got on the bus going to Manchester, I would have gone through Manchester to Piccadilly or the North Western bus staton.

What did you intend to do when you reached Piccadilly? —To meet a friend.

Who?—A man.

Who?—Lawson.

Who is Lawson?—He is a friend.

What does he do?—You mean for his living?

Yes?—He is a labourer.

Did you make arrangements to meet him?—No, no definite arrangements, but I knew where I could see him.

Did you want to see him?—Not particularly, but it came to my mind that I should see him.

Where did you intend to sleep when you left your parents' home?—If that bus had come through into Manchester I would likely have been able to get a bed in the Forces' Dormitory.

Why didn't you stay at home at New Mills?—I should think that would be obvious.

Would you answer my question?—Yes, I will, because I have a great respect for my mother and my home and, feeling as I was feeling and thinking as I was thinking that I had something wrong with me, I didn't want to stay and use one of their beds.

When you say 'thinking you had something wrong with you', you mean that you had venereal disease?—I do, yes.

Did the inspector then say to you, 'Do you care to tell me where you stayed on the Saturday night, 19 October'?—He asked me where I had stayed.

You asked him if he had seen your mother, didn't you?—Not in answer to his question.

Why did you ask him that?—Because I was concerned.

Did you want to be quite certain that your journey to New Mills had been discovered or not discovered?—No, I was not in the least worried.

Why did you ask?—Concern for my people. I didn't know how long Inspector Stainton had been looking for me and enquiring for me. I thought perhaps he had been home and upset them at home.

He told you that he had not seen your mother, didn't he?—He did . . .

You did say, didn't you, that you had stayed at Grafton House in Hyde Road?—I did definitely. You see, sir, these questions were not asked me in the order that they were put on that paper. There were intervals between these questions.

In your statement written out and signed you said that you had been directed to Hyde Road, No 36?—Yes.

That is quite wrong, isn't it?—As I know it now, yes.

Now, let us see what the position is. On Sunday, 20 October, after this woman had died, you arrived at 36 Hyde Road?—On the Sunday?

Yes?—Yes, the Sunday evening.

And there you saw Mr Harris whom the jury have seen?

—That is quite true, yes . . .

Did you say that you were looking for work or had been directed to work at Seddons of Hulme?—That's quite true . . .

On 21 October, which was the Monday, you left Mr Harris at ten o'clock or thereabouts, didn't you?—Yes, I did.

Did you go at once to the Salvation Army hostel?—I walked round that way, yes . . .

Did Mr Reid of the Salvation Army hostel ask you where you had spent the night before?—I've heard him say he did. And if he says that he did, I accept that he did.

Did you stay at Sinclair's hotel?— I don't remember staying at Sinclair's hotel.

Do you think you did?—I doubt it very much.

Do you think that Mr Reid is wrong about that?—I think he's mistaken.

This much is quite clear. If you did say it, it was untrue. —Definitely. I don't see why the name Sinclair could be in my mind at all.

On 26 October, when you were at the Services' Transit dormitory, you were awakened by two police officers, were you not?—Yes, sir.

I gather you deny saying, 'You don't want me for murdering that fucking woman'.—I do deny that definitely.

Did you say, 'Is it about that coat?'—I did.

Do you regard it as curious that there are two statements by the policemen. One is wholly false and the other is true? —No, I am only speaking the truth. One remark that passed I did not say and the other I did say. I denied one and admitted the other. That is the simple truth . . .

Did you say 'I've got an uncontrollable temper'?—I did not.

You said that Mr Stainton put that to you?—He did.

Did you agree with him?—I said, 'That is not evidence'. That was my answer.

Were you agreeing that you had an uncontrollable temper? —I neither agreed nor denied it.

What do you say about it now? Have you?—I am on oath. I will speak the truth. Yes, I have.

I'm suggesting that just as you're saying so frankly now, you said so frankly then to the police officer?—You're definitely wrong, sir.

Did you then say this. 'It is possible that the hammer was got to do a job with'?—Yes.

Were you then seeking to explain that this hammer might have been bought for a purpose other than killing this woman?—I was not trying to explain nothing. The conversation, both questions and answers, was concerning this and that was one of my remarks. That was my remark after I had been shown the hammer and the conversation had been on the subject of the hammer.

Was that remark in point of time near to your remark, 'One cannot see what one does in the dark'?—No, sir. There was an interval between those two remarks.

This much is plain, isn't it? At the time you felt that had you contracted that disease from this woman, she deserved to be strangled?—I did not say she deserved to be strangled.

MR JUSTICE SELLERS: What did you say?—I said, my lord, that if I had known she had given me VD I would have strangled her . . .

You've heard the evidence about the turn-ups of your trousers?—Yes, sir.

You would agree, I suppose, that in order to get clinker and leaf material and so on, the material must be above the level of the turn-ups to get down into it?—I don't know, sir.

Don't you? You don't get it walking along flat ground do you?—You mean you get it sat down on flat ground.

Yes. D'you know how those five substances got into your trousers?—I don't know. I was not aware that they were there until I'd heard the evidence. There is one thing I do know and that is that they never came off that blitzed site in Deansgate because I was never on it.

Where is the man Slim?—I don't know, sir. I have been in custody since 26 October.

Have you tried to get hold of him?—No.

Re-examined by MR BURKE:

Is there any evidence which you have heard either before the magistrates or here that you were wearing a mackintosh that night?—None, sir . . .

It's been put to you that you have an uncontrollable temper. You've stated on oath that you have?—I have.

Without stating what they are, have you done things in the course of your life in temper for which you are sorry?—Yes, I have.

With regard to those things which you have done in your temper, and for which you are sorry, have you ever planned them out hours ahead?—Never.

Or have they been done on the spur of the moment?—In the heat of the temper, sir.

I don't want to go any further than this. Are those things, or some of them, within the knowledge of the police force?—They definitely are . . .

Are you in a position to explain to the members of the jury how it [the spot of blood] got there on the under part of your shoe?—I cannot explain how it got there. I may have walked in some spit or something. I may have walked in some spit from someone with a bleeding tooth or something . . .

Have you always claimed to be innocent of this crime?—I have, sir, and I claim it now.

Do you, on your oath, tell those members of the jury now that you did not murder this woman?—I definitely did not murder this woman, nor did I see her that day or that night.

Did you ever offer her violence of any kind?—Never.

NORMAN JONES, *police-sergeant in the Stockport Borough Police, examined by* MR BURKE, *said that between ten o'clock and quarter to eleven pm on Saturday, 19 October, he was on police duty and incidental to that duty he visited licensed houses in the town.*

MR BURKE: Is that a routine duty of the police force, the duty of visiting licensed houses?—Not exactly routine, sir. It's not a systematic part of my duty but it is a duty I carry out at my own discretion.

He said that he was in uniform and accompanied by police constable Moores. He said that police officers of the Stockport police force visited licensed premises in the course of their duties and that when they did so they recorded the times. He said that he knew the Wellington Hotel at Stockport. He said that it was a public house in two parts, inasmuch as it was built at a point where there were two road levels. He said that you can enter the upper part of the hotel from a road called Wellington Road South and that the lower part emerged on to Mersey Square. He said that on 19 October at 10.32 pm he visited the Wellington Hotel with Constable Moores and that he entered at the upper door from Wellington Road South and emerged from the lower door into Mersey Square. He said that the licensing hours on weekdays ended at 10.30 pm.

Cross-examined by MR NIELD, *he said that it was an ordinary routine visit to licensed premises and that some public houses were visited every Friday and Saturday nights.*

MR NIELD: Are Fridays and Saturdays usually visiting nights?—They can be visited any night, sir, but one can rely that at weekends they are visited.

Have you frequently visited the Wellington public house on Fridays and Saturdays in other weeks?—Well, that is subject to my tour of duty.

Well, other officers?—Other officers would probably have done so.

Many weekends in the year?—I should say so, yes.

On 19 October did you see that man [Rowland] in the Wellington?—I did not, sir.

FRANK BEAUMONT, *of 81 Brunswick Street, Chorlton-on-Medlock, Manchester, examined by* MR BURKE, *said that he had a small white plate on his front door 'No Hawkers, No Circulars'. He said that he remembered the night of 19 October.*

MR BURKE: Do you or do you not recognise the man who is in the dock? The man Rowland.—I am not in great difficulty.

You have difficulty, do you?—I have not seen the man for eight weeks.

For eight weeks?—And he looks thinner to me and he is also wearing a different suit.

Did you see a man on the night of the 19th?—Do you mean did I see a man? Did a man apply for rooms at the house on the 19th?

Did anyone apply for rooms? Did you know who that man was? Who was it?—Walter Brotherton.

Walter Rowland?—Rowland, is it?

Had he stayed there before on any occasion?—Well, he recalled to me that he had stayed there a month or six weeks before for one night in company with another man.

You say he came and applied for rooms at your establishment on the night of the 19th?—Yes.

Are you in any doubt as to that date?—It was Saturday, the 19th . . .

Do you keep a visitor's book at your establishment?—Yes.

Is that the book? (*Produced*)—That is the book. (*Exhibit 38*) . . .

Did the man Rowland who came there that night put his name in the visitors' book?—Yes.

Do you see his name in that book?—Yes.

Were you present when he put his name in that book?—Yes, he signed it on the mantelpiece in the little room, where he was going to sleep, the middle room downstairs . . .

What time of night did this man arrive?—At about 11.15 to 11.20 pm.

Did he remain in then or did he go out?—As far as I can recollect he went out for a few minutes, not for very long.

Did he or did he not tell you where he was going?—Yes, he told me where he was going. He was going for the fish and chips.

Did you hand him something before he went out?—I have an impression I lent him a key . . .

How long do you say he was absent?—A very short time. He gave me the key back when he came in. I was just going to bed, you understand. I didn't stand about waiting.

When you went to bed, was the key in your possession or in his?—The key was in my possession.

Mr Beaumont, what time was it when you went to bed that night?—About twenty to twelve, I should think, It's difficult to be sure of the exact time . . .

The following morning did you go into his bedroom?—I think so, yes.

What?—Yes, I had a word with him the following morning.

I asked you, did you go into his bedroom?—Yes.

Did anybody else go into that bedroom at about the same time as you?—Probably he would be served with hot water. A young lady either went into the room or left it at the door or something or another. I don't think I actually saw her go in, but we know the routine . . .

At what time was it you went in?—Sometime between nine and ten. It was Sunday morning. We're not very fussy on Sunday morning about getting up.

When you went in, was this man in bed or out of bed?—When I saw him the following morning he was dressed. He had on a blue suit.

Did he have any mackintosh with him?—I saw no mackintosh . . .

Would you look at the book once more, Mr Beaumont. What is the date on the left hand side?—Of arrival?

Yes the arrival date?—19/10/46.

Who filled that in?—I did.

Is that in your writing, those figures?—19.10.46? Yes.

Would you look at the other side of the page. The day he departed?—Yes.

What date is put there?—The date is 19.10.46, but that is an error.

You say that's an error?—Yes, I didn't know it was disputed.

Would it have been possible for this man to have gone out that night?—D'you mean through the front door or through the back?

Any way . . . —It is not impossible, but it is hardly likely that he would be aware of it.

In cross-examination by MR NIELD, *he was asked:*

Could Rowland have left your house at any time during the time and returned without your knowledge?—Oh yes, he could have done that but, as I have said, he wouldn't be aware of the fact.

What do you say?—He would not have been aware of the fact that it was possible.

What do you mean?—He would not know the arrangements in my house. He had only been there one night . . .

Could he have left the house without your knowledge?—Yes.

And returned without your knowledge?—Yes.

Do you say that next morning, the day he did in truth leave, he was fully dressed when you went in?—He was fully dressed when I saw him and when I spoke to him.

Not in his singlet?—Not to my knowledge.

Re-examined by MR BURKE:

Mr Beaumont, have you got the slightest interest in this man?—Not at all—on the contrary.

If he left your premises on the night of 19/20 October without your knowing, how would it have been possible for him to have achieved that?—Well, as you know, unfortunately he was in the middle room downstairs. He was not in an upstairs room. The kitchen is not used owing to the shortage of fuel and the kitchen is not used for any purpose except service purposes. You could walk through the back door or—it sounds far-fetched—you could go out through the window but it would not be a very nice job.

You have told my lord and the jury that you retired for the night at about twenty to twelve?—Yes.

Was Rowland in the house or out of the house at that time to your knowledge?—He was in the house.

The last witness was a witness called Charles Wilfred Bolton, of 28 Clerk Street, Bury, but he was such an unsatisfactory witness that neither the prosecution nor the defence could rely upon anything that he said. So I have omitted all his evidence.

FOURTH DAY   *Monday, 16 December 1946*

MR BURKE *addressed the jury on behalf of Rowland.*

MR WINGATE-SAUL *addressed the jury on behalf of the Crown.*

MR JUSTICE SELLERS *summed up.*

The jury retired at 4.40 pm and returned into Court at 6.35 pm.

THE CLERK OF ASSIZE: Members of the Jury, who shall speak as your Foreman? Are you agreed upon your verdict?

THE FOREMAN OF THE JURY: We are.

THE CLERK OF ASSIZE: Do you find Walter Graham Rowland guilty or not guilty?

THE FOREMAN: Guilty.

THE CLERK OF ASSIZE: You find Walter Rowland is guilty and that is the verdict of you all?

THE FOREMAN: Yes.

THE PRISONER: May God forgive you. You have condemned an innocent man.

THE CLERK OF ASSIZE: Walter Graham Rowland, you have been convicted of murder upon the verdict of the Jury. Have you anything to say why sentence of death should not be passed according to law?

THE PRISONER: Yes, I have, my Lord. I have never been a religious man, but as I have sat in this Court during these last few hours the teachings of my boyhood have come back to me, and I say in all sincerity and before you and this Court that when I stand in the Court of Courts before the Judge of Judges I shall be acquitted of this crime. Somewhere there is a person who knows that I stand here today an innocent man. The killing of this woman was a terrible crime, but there is a worse crime been [sic] committed now, my Lord, because someone with the knowledge of this crime is seeing me sentenced today for a crime which I did not commit. I have a firm belief that one day it will be proved in God's own time that I am totally innocent of this charge, and the day will come when this case will be quoted in the Courts of this country to show what can happen to a man in a case fo mistaken identity. I am going to face what lies before me with the fortitude and calm that only a clear conscience can give. That is all I have got to say, my Lord.

THE JUDGE'S CLERK: My Lords the King's Justices do strictly charge and command all persons to stand up and keep silence whilst sentence of death is passed upon the prisoner at the bar upon pain of imprisonment.

MR JUSTICE SELLERS: Walter Graham Rowland, the Jury have found you guilty of murder. The sentence of the Court upon you is that you be taken from this place to a lawful prison and thence to a place of execution and that you be there hanged by the neck until you be dead and that your body be afterwards buried within the precincts of the prison in which you will have been confined before your execution, and may the Lord have mercy on your soul.

IN THE COURT OF CRIMINAL APPEAL   No 908/46

ROYAL COURTS OF JUSTICE

Monday, 27 January 1947

BEFORE

THE LORD CHIEF JUSTICE OF ENGLAND
(Lord Goddard of Aldbourne)

MR JUSTICE HUMPHREYS

and

MR JUSTICE LEWIS

REX

v

WALTER GRAHAM ROWLAND

Mr Kenneth Burke and Mr H. Openshaw appeared as Counsel for the Appellant

Mr Basil Nield, KC, and Mr Bazil Wingate-Saul appeared as Counsel for the Crown

I

Monday, 27 January 1947

THE REGISTRAR: Is your name Walter Graham Rowland?
THE APPELLANT: Yes.

On this day an application for an adjournment for fourteen days was granted in view of the confession of David John Ware.

Monday, 10 February 1947

The Court refused the Appellant leave to call David John Ware but gave him leave to call two other witnesses, Henry Somerville and Walter Haydn Ellwood. Their evidence was as follows.

HENRY SOMERVILLE, *of 57 Rostherne Road, Adswood, Stockport, examined by* MR BURKE, *said that he remembered going to a cinema on 19 October. He did not know the date of his own knowledge but he knew it from the film. He had gone to the Plaza cinema, Stockport, which is in Mersey Square. The name of the film which he saw was 'Cornered'; the name of the star actor was Dick Powell. The cinema ended between 10.10 and 10.15 pm. When he went out of the cinema he went to the lower Wellington for a drink. He went into the bar. There were about half a dozen men standing there and one lady behind the bar. Usually, he said, there were two ladies.*

MR BURKE: Did you hear one of those men who was in the bar ask one of those ladies for something?—Yes.

What did he ask for?—Cigarettes.

Did you hear her say anything to that man in reply?— She said she had none in the place.

Did one of the men who was standing there then say something to the man who asked for the cigarettes?—Yes, there was a man who offered to sell him a packet.

Did he sell him a packet of cigarettes?—Yes.

Did you have cigarettes?—I had just a few but seeing him sell the cigarettes I asked him could he sell me ten and he did so for which I paid 10½d.

What sort of cigarettes were they?—Woodbines.

How many were in the packet?—Ten.

Do you know who the man was who sold you those cigarettes?—I think that man is in court today.

D'you know who it is?—Yes, Mr Rowland, here. (*Indicating.*)

Had you ever seen him since the time he sold the cigarettes until a fortnight ago when you appeared in this court?—No, never.

Were you able to identify him by means of a photograph shown to you by Mr Hinchcliffe?—Not exactly. I was able to identify him more in the flesh.

When did you first find yourself able to identify him as the man who sold you the cigarettes?—The last time he came here a fortnight ago.

MR JUSTICE LEWIS: You could not identify him from the photograph?—Not from the photograph.

MR BURKE: Was the photograph shown to you an ordinary photograph or a newspaper photograph?—It was an ordinary photograph.

Did you have any conversation with the two men you've just referred to—the man who sold you the cigarettes and the first man who bought the packet of cigarettes?—I don't remember that.

... At about closing time—by closing time I mean the time when the supply of drinks stops—is that 10.30 in Stockport? —Yes.

Do you remember anything happening with regard to the hand basin or the basin where the glasses are washed behind the bar?—Yes, I remember it overflowing.

Did you see any police officers on those premises that night?—Yes.

How many?—Two.

From which part of the premises did they come?—They came from the top, the upper Wellington.

By which door did they emerge from these premises?— The bottom.

About what time would that be when those officers came through the bar?—Between 10.30 and 10.35.

Did you on Sunday, 5 January, see a copy of the *News of the World* newspaper?—No, it wasn't on a Sunday, it was on the Monday night.

Was it the *News of the World* for 5 January 1947?—Yes, that's right.

I ought to have asked you. At what time did you leave

the bottom Wellington that night?—As near as I can say, 10.40.

Was Rowland still there or had he gone?—No, he had gone.

Did Rowland leave before closing time or after closing time, so far as you know?—Just after closing time.

You told my lords a moment ago that on Monday, 6 January, you saw the *News of the World* newspaper?—Yes.

Was that the newspaper for Sunday, 5 January of this year?—Yes.

Did you produce that newspaper when interviewed by Rowland's solicitor?—Yes.

And is that the newspaper? [*Same handed*]—That is the one.

Will you show my lords the article which attracted your attention?—(*the witness did so*).

Did you later communicate with the cashier of the firm which employed you and subsequently with Mr Hinchcliffe? —Yes.

Cross-examined by MR NIELD:

Can you tell my lord when you first saw Mr Hinchcliffe, the appellant's solicitor?—Stockport County was playing Bolton on the Saturday. Mr Hinchcliffe came and interviewed me the following Sunday.

MR JUSTICE LEWIS: Which Saturday?—The date was the time Stockport County played Bolton in the Cup.

LORD CHIEF JUSTICE: We don't know when that was. We want you to tell us the date?—It would be 12 January.

MR NIELD: The Saturday after you'd seen the notice in the newspaper?—Yes.

You were then shown a photograph by Mr Hinchcliffe? —Yes.

And you could not then identify the man?—I was not then certain.

But now you think that this is he?—Yes.

Can you help us about this? If someone leaves the lower Wellington soon after 10.30 can they be in Deansgate, Manchester, by motor car within ten or fifteen minutes?—I should say by motor car between fifteen and twenty minutes.

MR JUSTICE LEWIS: Are you differentiating between a motor car and motor bus?

MR NIELD: No. I was just going to ask about motor bus.

MR NIELD (*to the witness*): There is a bus service?—Yes.

That I suggest takes about seventeen minutes?—Yes. There is one at about a quarter to eleven, as far as I know. But he'd have a job to get there by eleven o'clock. It would take him all his time to get there by eleven o'clock.

MR JUSTICE LEWIS: If he got the 10.45 bus?—Yes.

LORD CHIEF JUSTICE: Mr Burke, I should very much like to see the photograph from which this witness failed to identify the prisoner.

MR BURKE: I understand that Rowland's solicitor borrowed it from a newspaper office to which in due course he had to return it.

[*The photograph was not produced.*]

WALTER HAYDN ELLWOOD, *of 33 Parkview, Cheadle Heath, Stockport, examined by* MR BURKE, *said that he was the manager of the Plaza cinema, Mersey Square, Stockport, and he produced the Board of Trade quota book kept by him in connection with the theatre. He looked at the entry for Saturday, 19 October, and it showed the name of the feature film as 'Cornered' and the name of the star actor as Dick Powell. He said that the performance finished on 19 October at 10.12 pm. He said that his cinema was about a minute's walk from the bottom Wellington hotel. It was just across the road.*

MR BURKE: How long do you think it would take to travel from Stockport by bus to Deansgate, Manchester?—You couldn't go to Deansgate, Manchester, by bus. You would have to go from Mersey Square to Piccadilly, then you would have to walk to Deansgate. If I were going to Deansgate I would get off at the Palace Theatre. I should think it would take me ten to twelve minutes walking to get across to Deansgate.

Is it at all possible to get from Stockport to Deansgate in a quarter of an hour by bus?—I should say impossible.

How long is your estimate of the time it would take?— I usually reckon twenty-five minutes in the morning.

To Deansgate?—No, to Manchester Palace. That is where I usually get off.

MR JUSTICE LEWIS: Do you change the programme every week?—Yes, an entire change on Sunday evening.

MR BURKE *addressed the Court on behalf of the Appellant.*
MR NIELD *addressed the Court on behalf of the Crown.*
MR BURKE *replied.*
THE JUDGES *conferred.*

THE LORD CHIEF JUSTICE: The Court has come to the conclusion that this appeal must be dismissed; but as a question has arisen here with regard to an application to call the evidence of a witness who is alleged to have made some confession with regard to this crime, and the Court has refused to allow that evidence to be given, the Court will put their Judgment into writing in order that they may deal fully with that part of the matter. That Judgment will be given at an early date, but the appeal is dismissed.

THE APPELLANT: I am an innocent man. This is the greatest injustice which has ever happened in an English Court. Why did you have the man who confessed here and not hear him? I am not allowed justice because of my past.

THE LORD CHIEF JUSTICE: Take him down.

THE APPELLANT: It would have knocked the bottom out of English law to have acquitted me and proved my innocence. I say now I am an innocent man before God.

17 February 1947

The judgment of the Court was read by MR JUSTICE HUMPHREYS.

[Anyone who wishes to read the whole judgment will find it starting on page 460 in Law Reports 1947 King's Bench.

The important parts of the judgment are those in which the Court gave its reasons for refusing to hear the evidence of Ware. This passage appears on p. 20 of my introduction and also on pp. 143–4, in the Report by Mr Jolly. The Court also said that in its view the evidence of Mr Somerville and Mr Ellwood would not have affected the minds of the jury.]

APPENDICES

	August		Ware joins the Army
	September		Rowland joins the Army
1943	July		Ware discharged from the Army on medical grounds, suffering from manic depressive psychosis
	November	15	Ware convicted of stealing and sentenced to six months' hard labour
1945	April	15	Ware convicted of stealing and sentenced to two months' imprisonment
1946	October	18	Ware runs away from the Salvation Army hostel in Stoke, where he has stolen money, and comes to Manchester
	October	18	Rowland meets Olive Balchin and says that he will see her on the following night
	October	19	5.40 pm. A man buys a hammer from Mac-Donald
			6.15 pm. Rowland catches bus to New Mills
			7.30–8 pm. Rowland arrives at his parents' house at New Mills
			9.15 pm. Rowland leaves his parents' house intending to take bus to Manchester
			10.30–11 pm. A man and two women (one of whom is identified subsequently by Mrs Copley as Olive Balchin) go into café near Deansgate, where Mrs Copley is a waitress
			12 midnight. Mercer sees man and woman quarrelling near bombed site at corner of Deansgate and Cumberland Street
	October	19/20	Between 11 pm (19 October) and 11 am (20 October) Olive Balchin murdered on bombed site
	October	20	11 am. Olive Balchin's body found
			Mercer identifies Olive Balchin as the woman he had seen quarrelling at midnight
	October	21	Ware surrenders to Sheffield police and confesses to the theft at Stoke. He is arrested
	October	26	11 pm. Rowland taken from the Services' transit dormitory to the Bootle Street police station. MacDonald identifies Rowland as the man who bought the hammer. Mrs Copley, with some hesitation, identifies Rowland as the man who came into café with Olive Balchin and another woman

			4.30 pm. Rowland charged with murder of Olive Balchin
	November	4	Mercer identifies Rowland at an identification parade at Strangeways Prison as the man whom he saw quarrelling with Olive Balchin at midnight
	December	12–16	Rowland tried for murder of Olive Balchin, convicted and sentenced to death
1947	January	22	Ware confesses to governor of prison to murdering Olive Balchin
	January	24	Ware makes detailed confession to Inspector Stainton
	January	27	Rowland's appeal comes before Court of Criminal Appeal and is adjourned for fourteen days
	February		Ware makes further detailed confession to Rowland's solicitor
	February	10	Rowland's application to call Ware to give evidence refused and his appeal dismissed
	February	17	Court of Criminal Appeal suggests that Home Secretary might order an enquiry into Ware's confession
	February	21	Home Secretary orders enquiry and appoints Mr J. C. Jolly, KC, to conduct it
	February	22	Ware withdraws his confession
	February	25	Mr Jolly reports that Rowland's conviction did not constitute a miscarriage of justice
	February	27	Rowland executed
1951	July	10	Ware attempts to kill a woman whom he did not know with a hammer which he had bought the same day
	July	13	Ware gives himself up to the police, confesses to the crime and is arrested
	November	16	Ware tried for attempted murder and found guilty but insane. Sent to Broadmoor
1954	April	1	Ware commits suicide in Broadmoor by hanging himself

APPENDIX 2

ENQUIRY INTO THE CONFESSION MADE BY DAVID JOHN WARE OF THE MURDER OF OLIVE BALCHIN IN RESPECT OF WHICH MURDER WALTER GRAHAM ROWLAND WAS CONVICTED AT MANCHESTER ASSIZES ON THE 16th DECEMBER, 1946

REPORT BY
MR JOHN CATTERALL JOLLY, KC

To The Right Honourable The Secretary of State
for the Home Department

You appointed me on the 21st February, 1947, 'to inquire into the confession made by David John Ware of the murder of Olive Balchin, to consider any further information which may have become available since the conviction of Walter Graham Rowland for the murder of Olive Balchin, and to report whether there are any grounds for thinking that there has been any miscarriage of justice in the conviction of Rowland for that murder.'

You further appointed Mr. Thomas Barratt, Superintendent of the Metropolitan Police Force, to be an assessor for the purposes of the inquiry. I have the honour to submit my report.

1. With Superintendent Barratt as assessor, and with the assistance of Inspector Hannam of the Metropolitan Police, I carried out the inquiry in Manchester on the 21st, 22nd and 23rd February.

2. Walter Graham Rowland, aged 38, was convicted at the Manchester Assizes on the 16th December, 1946, before Mr. Justice Sellers, of the murder in Manchester on the night of the 19th/20th October, 1946, of Olive Balchin, aged 40, and was sentenced to death, the Jury making no recommendation to mercy.

After the conviction of Rowland, David John Ware who was then detained in Liverpool Prison, made to the Governor of the prison a statement, dated the 22nd January, 1947, in relation to the murder, which was in the following terms: -

'SIR,

    I, David John Ware, wish to confess that I killed Olive Balshaw with a hammer, on a bombed-site in the Deansgate,

Manchester, on Saturday, October 19th, about 10 p.m. We had been to a Picture House near the Belle-Vue Stadium earlier in the evening. I did not know her before that night. I wish this to be used in evidence and accepted as the truth.

Signed

DAVID JOHN WARE.'

3. On the 24th of January, Ware was seen in Liverpool prison by Detective Inspector Stainton of the Manchester City Police Force. He was told by Detective Inspector Stainton that he was not obliged to say anything unless he wished to do so, but that whatever he did say would be taken down in writing and might be given in evidence. He thereupon made and signed the statement which is appended hereto (Appendix 2a). In that statement he reiterated that it was he who had committed the murder and he gave further details.

4. Rowland appealed against his conviction and the case came before the Court of Criminal Appeal on the 27th of January. The statements made by Ware were referred to and the hearing was adjourned to the 10th February. In the meantime Ware was seen in Liverpool prison by Rowland's legal advisers. He made the statement which is appended hereto (Appendix 2b). It consisted of replies to questions put to him by Mr. G. N. Hinchcliffe, Rowland's solicitor. Rowland's counsel were also present at the interview.

5. On the 10th February Rowland's appeal was again before the Court of Criminal Appeal and was dismissed. The Lord Chief Justice said: -

'The Court has come to the conclusion that this appeal must be dismissed; but as a question has arisen here with regard to an application to call the evidence of a witness who is alleged to have made some confession with regard to this crime, and the Court has refused to allow that evidence to be given, the Court will put their judgment into writing in order that they may deal fully with that part of the matter. That judgment will be given at an early date, but the appeal is dismissed.'

The judgment of the Court was later delivered by Mr. Justice Humphreys. In the course of the judgment Mr. Justice Humphreys said: -

'If we had allowed Ware to give evidence before us, and he had persisted in his confession of guilt, the Court would have been compelled to form some conclusion as to his guilt or innocence and to express that opinion in open court. In effect, therefore, the Court would have been engaged in trying not only Rowland, but also Ware and thereby usurping the function of a Jury. It is true that we should not be empowered to pronounce finally upon the issue of the guilt or innocence of Ware, who as the result of our judgment might have to stand his trial by Jury on this charge of murder. In that event, the findings of this Court could not fail to be prejudicial to his chance of an impartial trial. . . . Finally, we are not unmindful of the fact that there exists an authority in the person of the Home Secretary, who has far wider powers than those possessed by this court, who is not bound as we are by rules of evidence, and who has all the necessary machinery for conducting such an inquiry as is here asked for.'

6. During the course of my inquiry I, together with Mr. Barratt and Mr. Hannam, interviewed Ware and investigated the three statements which he had previously made. After persisting at first in maintaining that his former statements as to the murder were correct, Ware admitted that they were false, saying 'I'd better turn it in.'

A statement in writing was then taken from him by and in the presence of myself and Superintendent Barratt and written down by Inspector Hannam. Upon the completion of the statement it was read over to him and signed by him. That statement is appended hereto (Appendix 2c). The opening paragraph of the statement is as follows:-

'I wish to say that the statements I have given confessing to a murder are absolutely untrue. I have never seen the woman Balchin, who was murdered in Manchester, in my life. I did not murder her and had nothing whatever to do with the murder. I made these statements out of swank more than anything, but I had a feeling all along that I wouldn't get very far with them. My health has not been too good since the outbreak of war and I really do feel I want some treatment. I also thought I was putting myself in the position of a hero. I wanted to see myself in the headlines. In the past I wanted to be hung. It was worth while being hung to be a hero, seeing that life was not really worth living.'

The last paragraph is as follows:-

'I would like to say that I am sorry I have given the trouble I have and I didn't realise the serious consequences it might entail had the confession been believed.'

This last part of the statement was made after he had been expressly asked if there was anything that he wished to add.

7. I have considered this written statement in the light of the whole of my investigations and all the circumstances of the case and of my observation of Ware's manner, demeanour and mentality. I am satisfied that when Ware told me that he did not commit the murder he was then speaking the truth.

8. To carry the matter further I arranged for an identification parade. The Governor of the prison at my request proceeded to a cell and said to Ware, 'Ware, I am going to take you out now to an identity parade.' Ware replied, 'Yes, sir.' The Governor then said, 'There are ten other prisoners there, and I am going, first of all, to take you to where these ten men are and you can stand anywhere you like with them and then from that place we will take you to where the parade is held so that you are completely at liberty to stand where and how you like amongst those men. Is that all right?' Ware replied 'Yes, sir.'

The prisoner, Ware, then joined the file of ten men in the prison, chose where he would stand among them, and the file was marched into the prison yard. Throughout the whole of the subsequent proceedings Mr. Burke, Rowland's counsel, and Mr. Hinchcliffe, his solicitor, were present. I had previously explained to the witnesses concerned that a man called Ware had stated that it was he who had bought the hammer and killed Olive Balchin. When the parade was ready the first witness, Mr. Mac-Donald, was brought into the yard. Thereupon I addressed Mr. MacDonald as follows: -

'Mr. MacDonald, you have already stated during the course of these proceedings that a man bought a hammer in your shop on the 19th October at about twenty minutes to six.'

Mr. MacDonald replied: -
   'That is right.'
I then said: -
   'You have stated that man is the man Rowland.'
Mr. MacDonald replied: -
   'Yes sir.'
I then said: -
   'Now I want you to walk along the line where those men are standing, and tell me whether you see anyone there who in any way resembles the man Rowland whom you have already identified as being the man who bought the hammer in your shop on the 19th October. You understand?'
Mr. MacDonald said: -

'I understand perfectly.'

He then inspected the parade and having done so, said without any hesitation: -

'Nobody there I can recognise, sir.'

The witness Mr. Mercer was then brought to the parade, and after reminding him of his evidence at the trial of Rowland I said to him: -

'I am now going to ask you to walk along that line of men there and tell me whether you see anyone who you say was quarrelling with the woman on the 19th October at about midnight at the spot I have mentioned. Is that quite clear?'

Mr. Mercer replied: -

'Yes, sir.'

Mr. Mercer having inspected the parade said: -

'No—nothing like them.'

The witness, Mrs. Copley, was then brought to the parade. I directed her mind to the evidence which she had given on the trial of Rowland, and said to her: -

'I want you to walk along this line of people and when you have done so tell me whether you see anyone there who, you say, in any way resembles the man in your café on the occasion in question with the two women. Do you follow?'

Mrs. Copley said: -

'Yes, sir.'

Mrs. Copley having inspected the parade said: -

'No—no, definitely no.'

9. The parade then dismissed with the exception of Ware, who was taken to a room in the prison where in the presence of myself, Superintendent Barratt, Inspector Hannam, Mr. Burke and Mr. Hinchcliffe, each of the witnesses in turn was confronted by him.

Mr. MacDonald was first brought into the room and I said to him, indicating Ware: -

'The man standing over there is one of the men who was outside on the parade and is the man who has made the statement I am now investigating. Is he, or is he not, the man who bought—'. At this point Mr. MacDonald interposed 'Not the man.'

I continued with the words: -

'the hammer on the 19th October?'

and Mr. MacDonald said: -

'He is not the man—nothing like him.'

Mr. Mercer was then brought into the room, and I said to him: -

'Mr. Mercer, the man standing over there is one of the men who was on the parade just now outside and he is the man who has made the statement which I am now investigating. I want to ask you this question—Is he, or is he not, the man who was quarrelling with the woman on the 19th October about midnight at the corner of Cumberland Street and Deansgate in Manchester?'

Mr. Mercer replied: -

'Definitely no.'

The witness Mrs. Copley was then brought into the room and I said to her: -

'Mrs Copley, can you see the man standing over there? He is one of the men who was on the parade which has just taken place outside. He is the man who has made the statement which I am now investigating. Will you tell me: Is he, or is he not, the man who was in your café on the 19th October between half-past ten and eleven with two women?'

Mrs. Copley replied: -

'No he was not.'

I said: -

'He was not?'

And she replied: -

'No, definitely.'

10. The matters to which I have already referred appear to me to be conclusive, but there are other additional considerations which seem to me inevitably to lead to the same result.

11. At the trial of Rowland the witness, Mercer, stated that he saw a man and a woman quarrelling at about midnight on the 19th October at the corner of Cumberland Street and Deansgate. This corner adjoins the site upon which the murder was committed. Not only did the witness, Mercer, identify the man as being Rowland, but moreover on the 20th October before he had identified Rowland, he went to the Platt Lane Police Station mortuary, where he saw the body of a woman whom he recognised as being the woman he had seen the night before quarrelling with a man. That woman was Olive Balchin.

Ware in his first statement said that he committed the murder at about 10 p.m. If that statement were true it would follow that the witness Mercer was mistaken not only in identifying Rowland, but also in identifying Olive Balchin as being the woman whom he saw at midnight.

12. During the course of my inquiry I had a statement from a man called Wilfred Gosling, who is the licensee of the Sawyers Arms, Deansgate, Manchester. That information was in the

possession of the police before the trial of Rowland, but was clearly not material to any issue which arose at the trial. It is, however, now of importance. Mr. Gosling made a statement to me, and Mr. Burke and Mr. Hinchcliffe were present when he made it. The statement was to the following effect: On the 19th October he left his home roughly about 10.30 p.m. with his dog and went to the waste ground where the murder was committed, and stayed there for about five minutes. His dog ran over the waste ground and he wandered about and let the dog play. His dog is, in his precise words, 'rather a vicious dog'. I said to him during the course of his examination by me: -

'If a woman had been wounded—with blood on her—'
He then interposed and said: -

'It' (meaning the dog) 'would not have left that place.'
I said: -

'You are quite sure about that?'
and he answered: -

'No doubt in my mind.'

It is, of course, clear that if Olive Balchin had been killed by Ware at about 10 p.m. her body must then have been lying on the site at the time when the dog was running about there. I should add that Mr. Gosling also said to me that he rang up the police the next morning because he was sure his dog would not have left that spot 'if there had been anything', and he thought his statement might be of some assistance to them as regards time.

13. With reference to Ware's three statements confessing to the crime, I think it may not be without significance to note that in his third statement he introduced details to which he had made no reference before.

As regards the reasons given by Ware for the murder of Olive Balchin, in his statement to Detective Inspector Stainton he said 'We were quite close to each other, and being so near she took the opportunity of going through my pockets. I was aware of this but did not show her.' Later on in that statement he said, 'I made no attempt to get my money.' In the statement made to Rowland's solicitor, Mr. Hinchcliffe on the 31st January, Ware stated, 'After I had felt this woman feeling in my pockets I felt in my trousers cash pocket and found that a ten-shilling note, which I was certain I had put in that pocket, had gone.'

Dr. Murdoch, the Medical Officer of Liverpool prison, stated to me at an interview with me that Ware had told him that after he had struck the woman with the hammer 'he took this ten-shilling note from her and threw it at her as she lay on the ground and ran away.'

In fact, when Olive Balchin's body was found there was discovered a ten-shilling note in the left-hand bottom pocket of her overcoat. This note was carefully folded into a small capacity and placed at the bottom of a Midland Bank paper cash packet. On the top of the ten-shilling note there were 8 half-crowns, 1 two-shilling piece, 1 shilling, 1 sixpence, 1 penny and 2 half-pennies, making a total of £1 13s. 8d. The cash bag was then filled up with letters and bed tickets. It was placed at the bottom of the pocket and the pocket was then filled up with papers and other property. Had Olive Balchin stolen the ten-shilling note in the circumstances described by Ware, it could not possibly have been found where it was in fact found, unless, of course, there was some other ten-shilling note which has not been discovered.

14. As to the details in Ware's three statements in which he said that he had committed the crime, I am satisfied that they are such as could have been derived from newspaper reports, statements inserted at the instance of the police, discussions with prisoners who were received in prison after the murder, and from his own imagination. Although Ware was in custody on charges of larceny and fraudulent conversion from the 21st October and was sentenced to imprisonment at the Stoke-on-Trent Quarter Sessions on the 15th January, 1947, he would have, while awaiting trial, access to newspapers. Inspector Hannam made certain investigations on my instructions, and as a result of these gave me the following instances of matter which had appeared in the Press. He said: -

'I have inspected numerous Press cuttings published prior to the committal of Rowland. One of those includes at the request of the police a photograph of the coat worn by Balchin and comment is made of the distinctive nature of the buttons upon that coat. In at least two of these reports the price paid at the time the hammer was purchased is quoted, and one sets out in thick type the finding some distance from the body of the piece of paper in which the hammer was wrapped, and deals with the hammer impressions on it. In two of these Press cuttings which appeared quite early after the discovery of the body the name of the victim is said to be " Balshaw." In one of these cuttings published within a few days of the discovery of the body there reads the sentence, "there were severe injuries to the head and the nail of the index finger of the left hand was missing."

K

In yet another cutting on the 6th November, 1946, the following sentence appears, "her right cheek-bone was broken in two places, the injuries having been caused by many blows." '

It is noteworthy that in the first and second of his statements Ware described the woman as Olive 'Balshaw,' which is a name by which she was described in the Press paragraphs mentioned above.

15. In the course of the interview to which I have referred, Ware, before he admitted that his statements of guilt were false, said that he purchased the hammer about 4 o'clock. That statement was, of course, clearly inconsistent with the evidence of the witness, MacDonald, at the trial.

16. In his written statement made at my inquiry Ware said that during the afternoon of the 19th October he went to a cinema alone. He said that the picture which he saw was to the best of his memory a war-time picture with aeroplanes and parachutists jumping out. He was tired and had a sleep whilst he was in the pictures. He was on the ground-floor in a seat for which he had paid 2s. 9d. There was a clock on the right-hand side of the screen which he noticed was half-past five when he woke up and he decided to pull himself together and go out.

On my instructions, Ware was taken in a police car to Woolworth's shop in Piccadilly, Manchester, and from there he directed Inspector Hannam to the cinema which he said was the one he entered on the afternoon of the 19th October. Inspector Hannam has caused enquiries to be made as to the pictures showing in the cinema on that afternoon, and the main picture was 'Theirs Is The Glory,' which depicted the battle of Arnheim [sic] showing aeroplanes and parachutists. Ware had previously mentioned in conversation with me that he thought the scene of the picture was Holland. Inspector Hannam also ascertained that the cheapest price of admission to that cinema is 2s. 9d., and that the seats at this price are on the ground-floor.

It appears to me to be extremely significant that this was the first time Ware ever said anything about going to the cinema in the afternoon (as distinct from the evening) of the 19th October and that upon being checked his statement is consistent with the ascertained facts.

17. In his statement made at my inquiry Ware said that after leaving the cinema he retraced his steps to Piccadilly and had some tea at a café. He left the café at about 7 o'clock, and went to the Oxford Public House in Oxford Street, Manchester, where

he remained until closing-time (which was in fact 10 p.m.). He caught a bus to Stockport and went to Richard's lodging house, number 7, Great Egerton Street. Inspector Hannam has made certain enquiries, and he gave me the result of his enquiries in the following terms:-

'I went to-day to Richard's Lodging House, number 7, Great Egerton Street, Stockport, and there interviewed the proprietress, Mrs. Dean, and an old gentleman named Ernest Plant who is in charge of bed booking. Following the inspection of the lodging house register by the police subsequent to Ware's confession, the book was destroyed' (by the proprietor) 'but Mr. Ernest Plant pointed out to the police officers the entry made in that book on the 19th October, 1946, showing that Ware slept on the premises on that night. He remembers Ware's arrival because, having asked him where he came from, there was a joke over the spelling of his surname and that of the word "where." He says the man occupied bed 31, which I also inspected and found it to be at right-angles to all the other beds in the room in which it was situated. To the best of Plant's recollection, Ware arrived at the lodging house on the 19th of October between 11.15 and 11.30 p.m. and he produced his identity card.'

Ware had mentioned in his written statement made at my inquiry that he produced his identity card and that he occupied a bed which was turned at right-angles to other beds.

My belief is that Ware, realising that the time of his arrival at Stockport could be checked, was obliged to fix the time of the murder which he was saying he had committed, at an hour which would be consistent with his journey to Stockport and arrival there. It follows also that at the time which the witness Mercer indicated as the time when he saw the man and the woman quarrelling at the corner of Deansgate and Cumberland Street, Ware was in fact at the lodging house at Stockport.

18. Dr. James Brierley Firth, the Director of the Home Office Forensic Laboratory at Preston, made a statement to me in the presence of Mr. Burke and Mr. Hinchcliffe. He examined Ware's clothing at the end of January. He stated that there was no evidence of bloodstains on Ware's trousers. An appreciable amount of material was obtained from the trouser turn-ups and this was essentially the usual type of fibre stuff commonly found in trouser turn-ups, and the quantity indicated that the trouser turn-ups had not been brushed for a considerable time. He stressed the marked contrast which he said there was between

this material and the material found in Rowland's trousers to which he had deposed at Rowland's trial. His statement may be summarised in the following words which he used: -

'From my observations in this case, I am of the opinion that the description given by Ware of his attack on the deceased is not consistent with the facts in this case. There is no evidence from his clothing that he was ever on the site under the conditions described by him.'

19. At Rowland's trial, one of the suggestions on the part of the prosecution was that Rowland had heavily greased his hair in order to darken it. I had before me during my inquiry the statement of Mrs. Ida Hollenshade, who lives at 36, Hyde Road, Ardwick, and is the part-owner of an hotel there. She made her statement to me in the presence of Mr. Burke and Mr. Hinchcliffe. In her statement she said that Rowland had stayed at her hotel on the night of Sunday, 20th October. I asked her why she particularly remembered that night, and she replied as follows: -

'I particularly remember that night because I grumbled about the grease and that on my pillow slips because my men if I see them with a greasy head, I always give them a piece of calico to put on the pillows.'

I then asked her: -

'In which room do you mean? Do you mean Rowland's?' She replied that she did.

I asked her: -

'Was it a substantial amount of grease?' to which she replied that she was very 'steamed up' about this pillow slip and, as he had asked to stay that night, she told him to come into the kitchen and she would give him an old piece of calico to put on the slip.

20. Dr. Murdoch, the Medical Officer at Liverpool prison, had an interview with me. He told me that Ware was first admitted to Liverpool prison on, he thought, the 22nd October from Stoke. As a result of Ware's making his statement to the Governor saying that it was he who had killed Olive Balchin, he was admitted into hospital. When interviewed by Dr. Murdoch in the usual course of his duties, he said that he had been discharged from the Army at a time when he was depressed. To Dr. Williams, the Deputy Medical Officer, he said that he had confessed to a murder in Edinburgh. To Dr. Murdoch he stated that he did not confess to a murder, but intended to murder a girl at Falkirk. He was 'put about' when he was asked why he

should confuse Falkirk with Edinburgh. He said that he was at Larbert before he was discharged from the Army. He denied at first to Dr. Murdoch that he had had access to any newspapers whilst he was on remand, but eventually admitted that he had had access all the time, but significantly, as I think, he denied that he had ever read about the Rowland case.

Dr. Murdoch formed the view that Ware was a man who was 'attempting a hoax' and that he realised that he would not himself be in any danger 'because witnesses had already proved someone else had done it and they could not touch him.'

21. There are certain facts in connection with the medical history of Ware which seem to me of importance. In July, 1941, he was admitted to the Buckinghamshire Mental Hospital from which he was discharged after three weeks. In August, 1942, he was called up for military service, but in July, 1943, was discharged on medical grounds. His Army medical record shows that in 1943 he stated to the Army doctors that he had had a tendency to be depressed since his youth. According to Ware, he liked the Army at first, but since February of 1943 he had lost interest in work, friends and recreation. When he was discharged from the Army in 1943 the diagnosis was manic depressive psychosis.

22. I have already referred to the written statement which was taken from Ware by myself and Superintendent Barratt. During the conversation that preceded the taking of the written statement, Ware said, amongst other things, that he started reading about murders and was interested in them when he was a schoolboy. He said that he was interested in the Heath case, Sidney Fox and Rouse. He said he remembered that Rouse insured himself, burnt a body in a car, and made believe that the burnt body was his own. He said that Fox was a similar case, that he insured his mother and set fire to a bedroom at Brighton. He referred also to the case of Armstrong.

I regard these matters, taken with the other material before me, as some indication of a morbid interest in the macabre, which might well for exhibitionist reasons lead a man to assume responsibility for a murder which he had not committed.

23. There is one further point I must add. Together with the Governor of Manchester Prison and Superintendent Barratt, I had an opportunity of seeing Rowland. I did not think there was anything in his appearance which was at all likely to lead to his being mistaken for Ware. I observed a definite difference in physique, in the shape of face and in the nose. These impressions were shared by Superintendent Barratt.

24. Having enquired into the confession made by David John

Ware of the murder of Olive Balchin, and having considered further information which has become available since the conviction of Walter Graham Rowland for the murder of Olive Balchin, I report that I am satisfied that there are no grounds for thinking that there has been any miscarriage of justice in the conviction of Rowland for that murder.

25. I feel that I should express my deep appreciation of the co-operation of Superintendent Barratt and Inspector Hannam in this heavy and responsible duty.

J. CATTERALL JOLLY.

25th February, 1947.

APPENDIX 2a

Liverpool

24th January, 1947

I, David John Ware, have been told by Detective Inspector Stainton that I am not obliged to say anything unless I wish to do so, but that whatever I do say will be taken down in writing and may be given in evidence.

(Signed) DAVID JOHN WARE.

'I left stoke on Friday Oct. 18th 1946 with money that I had stolen from the Salvation Army Hostel where I worked as booking Clerk.

I hurried to Longton where I caught a bus to Uttoxeter & from there by Train to Manchester. Arriving in Manchester about 7.30 pm. I met a girl & stayed the night with her in some part just outside the City. On Saturday morning I left her & wandered around on my own scheming how I could get some more money. I decided in the Afternoon to by a Hammer for purpose of committing robbery with violence.

I bought a hammer after some searching near the railway station which is on the road from Piccadilly leading to Manchester Hippodrome. I tried many shops in this area but they could not oblige me.

At six pm I met Olive Balshaw outside the Hippodrome I spoke to her & suggested going to the pictures my idea was to kill time till it got dark.

I went to a small Picture House near the Belle Vue stadium with her. We came out at 9.0 pm had a cup of coffee opposite the cinema & caught a bus to the centre of the City.

I did not know whether to leave her or not but after finding a dark place not far from Piccadilly I decided to spend a while with her. The spot where we stopped was a place or building that I took to be bombed in this war. We went inside the ruins & stood for a short while near the entrance. We were quite close to each other & being so near she took the opportunity of going through my pockets. I was aware of this but did not show her. I was ate* up with hatred & felt immediately that I'd like to kill her. I realised I had the hammer so suggested that I'd like to make water & went further in the building. In there I took the brown paper off the hammer & threw it in the corner.

I went back to her & suggested moving further inside where we could not be seen. She agreed to this & we moved further inside. She was on my left & with my right hand I got the Hammer out of my pocket. While she was still in front & had only a few paces to go before reaching the wall I struck her a violent blow on the head, (I should say the right side). She screamed & before she† her scream lasted any length of time I

*Ware's initials inserted above this word.

†Ware deleted this word and initialled the deletion.

struck her again this time she only mumbled. Her hands were on her head protecting it the second time she fell to the floor up against the wall & I repeated the blows. Blood shot up in a thin spray. I felt it on my face & then I pannicked threw the hammer & left everything as it was. I made no attempt to get my money. I ran & ran zig-zag up & down streets I didn't know eventually getting to Salford Station. I was frightened of going on the station so decided to go to Stockport I caught bus to the Hippodrome then another to Stockport, sleeping at a lodging House there. On Sunday I tramped to Buxton & on to Chapel en le frith where I stayed the night at the institution. On Monday I Hitch Hiked to Sheffield & surrendered to the Police for the stealing of the money at the Stoke on trent salvation Army Hostel.

I have been in custody since.'

(Signed) DAVID JOHN WARE.

I have read over the above statement.

(Signed) DAVID JOHN WARE.

Witness:

(Signed) F. STAINTON.

(Signed) DOUGLAS NIMMO
Det. Cons.
Manchester City Police.

Detective Inspector.
Manchester City Police.

APPENDIX 2b

DAVID JOHN WARE says: -

I am at present serving a term of imprisonment in H.M. Prison, Walton, Liverpool.

The statement I made to Detective Inspector Stainton of the Manchester City Police Force on the 24th January, 1947, is true.

I am a stranger to Manchester, having only visited the City on two occasions previous to the 19th October, 1946, when I was there about two or three hours each time.

When I arrived in Manchester from Stoke-on-Trent, on the 19th October, 1946, I had about £1 5s. in my possession.

I bought the hammer referred to in my statement of the 24th January at a Shop which was situate on the main Road from the Railway Station to the Hippodrome Theatre. The Shop was on the left hand side of the road some little distance after passing under the bridge which passes over the Road below the Railway Station. The Road declines from the Railway Station and a little further down from the shop it inclines to the Manchester Hippodrome.

In the window of the Shop there were a number of what appeared to be second hand tools displayed for sale.

Whilst I was buying the hammer a man came in and bought a screw driver. He was served whilst the Shopkeeper was attending to me.

I paid 3s. 6d. for the hammer. The man who served me was of stocky build and middle aged. The hammer was a double-headed hammer and I took it to be a cobblers hammer. After buying it I said to the man who supplied it, 'This will be suitable.' He wrapped it in a piece of brown paper.

After meeting the woman at the Hippodrome Theatre, we got on a tram car the indicator of which read 'Belle Vue.' We left the tram car at the Stadium and then walked up the road for quite a long way until we came to a third-rate Picture House on the right hand side of the road. We went into the Picture House together.

The woman was wearing a light brown Tam O'Shanter type of hat. I am certain of that. Her coat was either dark blue or dark brown. It was of the double-breasted type. The buttons on the coat attracted my attention. They somehow appeared to me to be unsuitable to the coat.

On returning to Manchester we left the bus at Piccadilly.

We walked forward until we came to the Shops down the road to the left and then turned to the right eventually coming to the bombed ruin. I was looking for a quiet place.

After I had felt this woman feeling in my pockets, I felt in my trousers cash pocket and found that a 10s. note, which I was certain I had put in that pocket, had gone.

After I left the bombed site, I found myself at a Railway Station. I thought of going on to the Station, and asked an elderly man what Station it was and he told me it was Salford Station.

I became afraid of going on to the Station and I got on a tram car close by. I asked the Guard if I was going to the Hippodrome. He said 'No' and pointed out to me the Buses at the Bus Station.

I boarded a bus and took a ticket for the Hippodrome. On the bus I noticed spots of blood on the left sleeve of my macintosh.

When I got to Sheffield I took the belt off my macintosh and threw it away together with my cap. I did this in order to alter my appearance. I later read in the newspapers that the man wanted for killing the woman in Manchester had not been wearing a hat and I realized I had made a mistake in throwing my cap away.

I surrendered myself to the Sheffield Police for the Offence I had committed at Stoke as a 'cover up.' I thought I would be safer from possible detection in the hands of the Police or in prison, than I would be if I were wandering about.

Whilst on remand before my conviction I had access to newspapers, I read all about the finding of the woman's body but did not read any report of either the Police Court Proceedings or the trial of Rowland. The last I read was a paragraph which said that an arrest in connection with the Manchester 'Blitz Site Murder' was expected at any moment.

I then purposely avoided reading the newspapers, as I did not want to read anything more about the murder.

The first thing I heard of Rowland's conviction was on Saturday the 18th January 1947.

On that day whilst at Exercise in Walton Prison a fellow Prisoner told me that a man who had been convicted of the Murder of a woman at Manchester had Appealed and that his Appeal had been dismissed.

This information worried me a great deal as I knew that only a short time would elapse before that man's execution. I thought a great deal about it and on Wednesday the 22nd January 1947

I asked to see the Governor of the Prison and I made a statement to him.

I do not know the man Rowland.

APPENDIX 2c

H.M. Prison
Strangeways
Manchester
22nd February, 1947

STATEMENT OF DAVID JOHN WARE, PRISONER NUMBER 7305

'I wish to say that the statements I have given confessing to a murder are absolutely untrue. I have never seen the woman Balchin, who was murdered in Manchester, in my life. I did not murder her and had nothing whatever to do with the murder. I made these statements out of swank more than anything, but I had a feeling all along that I wouldn't get very far with them. My health has not been too good since the outbreak of War and I really do feel I want some treatment. I also thought I was putting myself in the position of a hero. I wanted to see myself in the headlines. In the past I wanted to be hung. It was worth while being hung to be a hero seeing that life was not really worth living.

The first time I thought of confessing to this murder was when I read about it in the Daily Herald when I was at Buxton on the Monday after the murder. It was the twentyfirst. On that day I was already wanted by the Police at Stoke-on-Trent for stealing some money and I noticed that the description of the man wanted for the Manchester murder answered my description. I went on to Sheffield the same night and went into the Library. Before I went to the Library I went to the Salvation Army Hostel and I was worried because I was broke and had no money. I then realised it was the Salvation Army I had stolen the money from at Stoke and that they might have sent a message through about me and I might be arrested. I think I had eightpence halfpenny when I went in there and I spent that on tea and cakes and then left. It was then I went to the Library and I read in the papers about the murder. I then read the description of the man who it was said was wanted. I went to the Salvation Army Hall, not the Hostel, and told the officer there that I had stolen money from the Salvation Army Hostel at Stoke. I did this because I was tired and hungry and the Salvation Army Officer took me to the Police Station. On three previous occasions when I have committed offences I have given myself up to the Police. I made a statement about the offence I had committed and where I had been but I denied I had been to Manchester. I did not say anything about the murder; I was not prepared to confess to it then as I didn't know enough detail about it.

During my remand and whilst awaiting trial at Quarter Sessions I read all about the murder from the newspapers and continuously built up a story so that I knew all the details of it. It was during this time that I made up my mind to confess to the murder at a convenient time. During the first few days after the murder before anyone was arrested there didn't seem to be too much in it but after I knew Rowland was arrested for it, it magnified the thing and made it bigger altogether. I knew then there would be plenty of time for me to confess. I wanted him to be either sentenced to death or to make my confession just before he was hung so as to make it spectacular in the way I snatched him from the gallows. I set myself to get all the details of the murder in my mind and continuously repeated the story to myself until I knew it right off.

While I was awaiting my trial Rowland was sentenced to death and I read about it in the paper and I also read that he was going to appeal. I thought this was the right moment to come out with my confession so that it could get to the Court of Appeal. I was then in Liverpool Prison and after applying to see the Governor I made the confession to him. I wrote the confession out myself but I did not put any detail in it. The statement of confession which I wrote out and handed to the Chief Officer is untrue. I was then put into hospital in the Prison and the following Friday two officers from the Manchester C.I.D. came to see me. I told them certain details which I had prepared in my mind and then put it into a statement in writing for the Officers. This statement was also untrue and the matters which I stated I had learned from reading the newspapers and from conversation with other prisoners, some of whom came to the prison after the murder. I cannot name the prisoners with whom I discussed the murder apart from one being Frank—something —and another a Scotsman. I tried to get all the facts I could from other prisoners. I was rather surprised to find that so many people believed me but when I found they were I carried on with it. I also played on the fact that the real prisoner made such a strong claim to innocence. After this, in fact a week later, I was interviewed by a solicitor and two barristers who said they were representing Rowland. I made a statement to them also or really I answered questions that they asked me. They did tell me that I need not answer unless I wanted to. That statement and the answers I made to their questions were untrue. I feel much easier in my mind now that I have told the real truth. It was because I was so well fitted with the description of the man wanted for murder that I fell into this and chose it as the one to confess to.

On 19th of October I was in Manchester, arriving by train from Uttoxeter at 7.30 p.m. or thereabouts. I know it was 7 p.m. by the clock at Stockport Station as the train passed through it. I left the Station by the main entrance, down the slope to a public house at the bottom on the left hand side. I think the name of the public house had some connection with the railway. I really went in to the pub to change a lot of coppers and silver which I had stolen, into notes. There were too many people in the pub to safely do this so I left it and went to another public house about two hundred yards further along past the Station away from the City. In this pub, in the public bar was a short stoutish woman serving the beer. I changed my coppers and silver, I think about three pounds worth altogether, with this woman. I think I made the excuse it was money I had taken for newspapers. Whilst I was in there a man was put out of the bar by two men who I think were on the staff, after he had insulted the landlady. I think the time was then about a quarter past eight. Leaving this public house I went to Piccadilly and entered another public house where I stayed for drink until nearly closing time. I then went to a cafe opposite where there is a deaf woman in charge. It appeared to be visited by a loose type of woman. I left there at about eleven o'clock and sat on a seat in Piccadilly. A prostitute came and sat down beside me and I arranged to spend the night with her. We took a taxi for a short journey which I believe cost about three shillings and went to a residential hotel where the girl was known. I only knew the Christian name of the girl but I have forgotten it. The house was kept by a rather stout foreigner who I believe was Italian; I paid twenty-five shillings for our bed and breakfast and signed my correct name in the register. In the same hotel that night was a man with a scar on his right cheek aged about twenty-five, who was associating with a girl in the house. This man later came to Liverpool Prison where he was to commence serving a six months sentence. He had a Welsh girl in the house. I slept with my girl all night and got up about nine o'clock in the morning. We left the house a bit after ten o'clock, went to a shoe shop a few doors away, and to a cafe a few doors away from that for a

meal. We then both caught a 'bus with Piccadilly on it and went
to Piccadilly which was a three halfpenny ride. I think there was
a hospital near where I caught the 'bus. On reaching Piccadilly
we went into a rough public house in one of the side turnings
off Piccadilly and I left the girl there, it would be round about
half past twelve. I wandered round the blocks for a few minutes
and then decided to have some lunch. I went into Woolworth's
and got a meal of fish, potatoes and green peas. On leaving
Woolworth's I turned right and continued along that road for
some distance and got into a market where there was a number
of stalls. I then went to a posh cinema which was about five
minutes walk from Piccadilly. Between Piccadilly and the cinema
I passed a tableaux forming up; I think it was to do with the
Army as one of the things I saw outside the large building was
a large decorated model depicting a Military badge. There were
soldiers, nurses, and ambulance men congregating there also.
The cinema I went into was very near to this place and I paid
2s. 9d. for my seat which was well down on the ground floor.
I cannot recall the title of the picture but to the best of my
memory it was a wartime picture with aeroplanes and parachutists jumping out; there was nothing outstanding in the
programme which I can remember. I was tired and had a sleep
whilst I was in the pictures. There was a clock on the right-hand
side of the screen which I noticed was half-past five when I woke
up and I decided to pull myself together and go out. It would
be about 5.45 p.m. when I left. I retraced my steps to Piccadilly
and had some tea at Gardener's Cafe. I think I had sausages,
potatoes and peas. I left this cafe at about seven o'clock and
strolled easily to the Oxford public house in Oxford Street where
I entered the first room on the left inside the door. It has a
horseshoe shaped bar and I was at the left hand portion. I stood
at the bar for a time and then took a vacant seat at a table in
the same bar where there were two women and a man sitting.
I thought they were all together at first but later found they
weren't. The man was a demobbed soldier, I think from the
R.A.S.C., as he was talking about having his ninety pounds
gratuity and the women were pulling his leg about not buying
any drinks. The man was about twenty-six, 5 feet 8 inches, fair
hair, clean shaven, medium build, dressed in a greyish suit with
an Army Discharge raincoat. It looked like demob clothes and he
was very smart. From the conversation I judged that both women
were married and aged about 35 to 40. One had on a very light
coloured mackintosh with very large patch-pockets. We sat there
altogether for an hour and when no one bought them any drinks

they left. There was an old woman who came in and sat down and begged some cigarettes from me. The bar got very crowded indeed and I stayed talking to the man until the house closed. I had told him that I was a booking clerk. When we left the public house I left him immediately. I knew I should not get a bed in Manchester but knew I should get one at Stockport so I decided to get there whilst someone was up. I took a 'bus from nearby to the Hippodrome and from there took another 'bus to Stockport. Whilst I was on the latter 'bus I asked a man if I was all right for Stockport but he told me that I must get off at once as that 'bus turned the wrong way. I got off and changed on to another 'bus by walking a little way along the road to the next 'bus stop. I paid threepence for the journey. I did on the wrong 'bus and about sixpence on the following 'bus to Stockport. If I came out of the Oxford at ten thirty, which I believe was closing time, I would have been at the lodging house in Stockport at between 11.15 p.m. and 11.30 p.m. I do not know the name of the lodging house or the street it is in, but on going over the railway bridge entering Stockport I had to turn left and then left again. I had not been to that lodging house before. I saw an old man in charge of the house and he took me into a rough office and asked me if I had my identity card. I produced my identity card and I believe the man copied the particulars off it. The card was in my proper name and the old man wrote the particulars in a small book about 10 inches by 6 inches. The man told me that I had got the last bed and this was the first bed on the right in the first room on the first floor, this bed being turned at right angles to other beds. When I got to the lodging house a number of the residents were in the general room talking around a stove. I slept at this place and did not leave until about 8.30 a.m. the next morning or perhaps nine o'clock. I had break-fast at the Tramway depot canteen at Stockport. On this day I intended going to Stoke and endeavouring to influence them to do nothing about the money I had stolen. My money was very low and I got on the road and walked hoping to get a lift. After walking about six miles I found I was on the road to Buxton so I continued. I knew there was a workhouse where I could get a bed near Buxton and I stayed at the workhouse at Chapel-en-le-Frith. I left there next morning (Monday) and walked back to Buxton where I bought five Woodbine cigarettes and a Daily Herald newspaper. I read about the Manchester murder and this was the first I knew about it. I had seen a News of the World on Sunday but saw nothing in it about the murder. Having read of the murder and noticed the description of the suspect it struck me how much I was like him and I thought it strange, in view of the fact that I had been walking about, that I had not been stopped and questioned. I left Buxton to walk to Sheffield and I got two lifts on the road, one by a car and one by a small van which dropped me in Sheffield just as it was getting dark.

It was on this day that I thought of the idea of confessing to this murder and I decided to surrender to Sheffield Police for stealing the money at Stoke. I hoped the Police would also suspect me of the Manchester murder and in order to make my description more correctly fit the man wanted for murder, I threw away my cap so that I too should be hatless. To the best of my recollection I threw my cap and my belt from my raincoat away when in a small alley I think running beside a factory not far from the Salvation Army Hall at Sheffield. They were small buildings in the alley and I threw the belt which lodged on the roof and the cap I threw over the roof out of sight. The Sheffield Police did not directly question me about the Manchester murder although they did ask me to account for my movements on Saturday night. The cap was a brown tweed one, size $6\frac{7}{8}$, which I bought in Bolton and may have a Bolton shopkeeper's name inside. It was fairly new. The belt is a fawn ordinary raincoat type with leather covering on the buckle slightly worn. Regarding this cap and belt, whilst I think I am right in what I have said about the place when I threw them, I definitely had a cap and belt and definitely threw them away in Sheffield.

I do remember reading in the paper about the peculiarity of the buttons on the coat worn by the murdered woman.

While I was on remand and waiting trial I stitched mail bags to earn some money; in doing so I often pricked my fingers. I used to wear my raincoat whilst doing the mailbags and I accidentally got some spots of blood on the front of it. When I was preparing my mind to confess to this murder I deliberately put spots of blood on the lower forearm of the two raincoat sleeves. I later washed these spots off with a piece of wet rag and burnt some of them off with the tip of a cigarette. In my statement I made to the solicitor I referred to blood on the left sleeve of my macintosh but it is untrue what I continued to say about them. I said in the solicitor's statement that I paid 3s. 6d. for the hammer as I had been told this by a fellow prisoner.

It is true that I do not know much about Manchester having only been in the City, apart from this occasion, for one day in August last and for two days in 1943 when I stayed at Eccles and visited Manchester whilst I was there.

I would like to say that I am sorry I have given the trouble I have and I didn't realise the serious consequences it might entail had the confession been believed.

This statement has been read over to me and it is all true.'

(Signed) DAVID JOHN WARE.

Statement taken by and in the presence of Mr. J. C. Jolly, K.C., Superintendent T. Barratt and written down and read over by me.

(Signed) HERBERT HANNAM,
Detective Inspector.

22nd February, 1947.